G000291727

'Your affectionate and loving sister'

At the age of 19 Barbara Postlethwaite left the family home,
Denton Rectory in Norfolk, to marry a man 11 years her senior,
the Reverend Samuel Kerrich, and to start a new life at Dersingham
on the north western side of the county. She particularly missed
the company of her sister Elizabeth, from whom she was to be separated
for 19 years, from 1732-1751. Meetings were infrequent, and there
were none from 1741 to 1744. Fortunately they kept in touch by letter
and much of their correspondence has survived, covering topics as varied
as Richardson's novels, gardening, child-rearing and the matrimonial
fortunes of their friends. They exchanged views on the latest fashions, the
foibles of relations and servants, health, taxes and the weather. Major events
(with the exception of the '45 rebellion) scarcely touched their lives. Many
of the letters are taken up with the day-to-day preoccupations of family life
at this period. Others strike a more sombre note, for sickness, above all
the threat of smallpox, was an ever-present reality in
early eighteenth century England.
For all that, their conversational tone, warmth and intimacy, not only
reveal the distinctive personalities of the sisters, but also something
of a society where 'compared with men, we know little about what
women felt, thought and did'.*

*R. Porter, *English Society in The Eighteenth Century*
(Harmondsworth, Middlesex 1982), p.35.

Elizabeth Postlethwaite (1777)
Drawn in coloured chalk by her nephew, Thomas Kerrich
By courtesy of the National Portrait Gallery, London

'Your affectionate and loving sister':

the correspondence of
Barbara Kerrich and Elizabeth Postlethwaite
1733 to 1751.

Edited by Nigel Surry

The Larks Press

Published at the Larks Press
Ordnance Farmhouse, Guist Bottom
Dereham NR20 5PF
Tel/Fax 01328 829207

Printed at the Lanceni Press
Garrood Drive, Fakenham

October 2000

British Library Cataloguing-in-Publication Data
A catalogue record for this book is available
from the British Library

N.B. No part of the text or illustrations in this book
or on the cover may be reproduced without
written permission from the publisher

The publisher has been unable to trace the copyright of the
illustrations on pages 13 and 89

© Letters – The Master and Fellows of Corpus Christi College, Cambridge
Editorial and appendices - Nigel Surry 2000

ISBN 0 948400 92 7

PREFACE

This book, the correspondence of two sisters, Barbara Kerrich and Elizabeth Postlethwaite, is based upon their letters in the Parker Library at Corpus Christi College, Cambridge. Spelling and punctuation have been modernised. Dating in the correspondence is according to the modern style, i.e. the year is assumed to begin on 1st January.

I am grateful to the Master and Fellows for permission to have them published, and would like to express my thanks to the former Librarian, Dr F.W.Ratcliffe, the Assistant Librarian Mrs Gill Cannell, Ms Pat Aske, Senior Library Assistant and Mrs C.P.Hall, Library Archivist, who have made my visits to the Library so congenial.

I would also like to thank Dr John Alban, County Archivist of Norfolk, for allowing me to quote from documents in the Norfolk Record Office; and the staffs of Cumbria Record Office, Kendal, Portsmouth City Museums and Records Service, and Suffolk Record Office (Bury St Edmunds and Ipswich branches) for their help. I am equally indebted to the British Library and the Guildhall Library, London, the Norrish Central Library, Portsmouth, and Sudbury Library.

The following kindly agreed to the use of extracts from published works: Weidenfeld & Nicholson (The Orion Publishing Group Ltd), Mark Amory (ed.), *The Letters of Evelyn Waugh* (1980), p.195; Rogers, Coleridge and White, Literary Agents, Eva Figes, *Women's Letters in Wartime 1450-1945 (1993)*, p.9 (Pandora Press Imprint, Rivers Oram Press); Jonathan Cape (Random House Group Ltd), Gladys Scott Thomson, *Letters Of A Grandmother 1732-1735* (1944), p.53; William Plomer (ed.), *Kilvert's Diary 1870-1879 Selections from The Diary of The Rev. Francis Kilvert* (1944), p.38; B.T.Batsford Ltd (Chrysalis Books Ltd), Anne Buck, *Dress in Eighteenth Century England* (1979), pp.225-227.

Miss Rosemary Harden, Keeper of Collections (Costume) the Museum of Costume and Fashion Research Centre, Bath; Professor Roger Lonsdale of Balliol College, Oxford; Mrs Sally Barter, Norfolk Studies Library; Mrs Barbara Thompson of the Witt Library; Andrew Butterton, formerly of the V & A Picture Library; George Durrant & Sons (Halesworth Office); James Kilvington of the National Portrait Gallery Archive and Library; Simon Massen; Miss Susan Sloman of Agnew's, Miss Phillipa Taylor of King's Lynn Library and Tim Thorpe, Acting Curator, the Lynn Museum, were particularly helpful with specific enquiries.

Nor shall I forget the encouragement I received from David Coke, John Lowe, Janet Pennington and Malcolm Pinhorn. My final thanks go to Polly Burns who got me there and back. Was it better to travel than to arrive?

Nigel Surry
September 2000

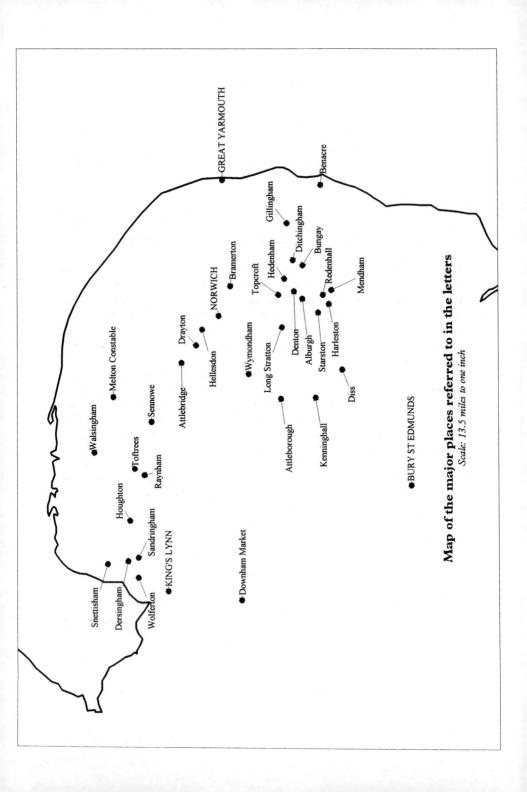

Map of the major places referred to in the letters

Scale: 13.5 miles to one inch

GREAT YARMOUTH

Benacre

Gillingham

Ditchingham

Bungay

Bramerton

NORWICH

Hedenham

Redenhall

Mendham

Topcroft

Drayton

Melton Constable

Hellesdon

Walsingham

Denton

Alburgh

Sennowe

Wymondham

Starston

Harleston

Toftrees

Long Stratton

Diss

Raynham

Houghton

Attlebridge

Attleborough

Kenninghall

Sandringham

BURY ST EDMUNDS

Snettisham

Dersingham

Wolferton

KING'S LYNN

Downham Market

LIST OF ILLUSTRATIONS

On the front cover: Denton Rectory and Gardens c. 1745

Francis Cufaude (oil on canvas)

Elizabeth Postlethwaite (1777)	facing title
Map of the major places referred to in the text	opposite
The Reverend Samuel Kerrich (1736)	facing p. 1
The Old Hall, Dersingham (1906)	p. 3
A View of the Church at Denton, Norfolk	p. 3
A carrier's cart outside a country inn	p. 13
Raynham Hall, Norfolk, seat of Lord Townshend (1779)	p. 21
A Fishing Party	p. 21
The Swan at Harleston (c.1900)	p. 25
Woman Standing and Man Standing	p. 28
The Gough Family (1741)	p. 33
The Game of Quadrille (c. 1743)	p. 33
Pamela in the custody of Mrs Jewkes (1745)	p. 45
The Duet (1749)	p. 52
Benacre Hall, Suffolk (1824)	p. 62
Houghton in Norfolk, seat of the Earl of Orford (1779)	p. 62
The Tuesday Market Place, King's Lynn	p. 66
The Wedding of Stephen Beckingham and Mary Cox (1729)	p. 81
An eighteenth century dairy	p. 89
The kitchen of a large country house in the eighteenth century	p. 89
Miss Hannah Norsa (1794)	p. 102
Strolling Actresses in a Barn (1738)	p. 102
Hochstetter's map of Norwich in 1789	p. 108
Faden's map of Dersingham and district in 1797	p. 121
Faden's map of Denton and district in 1797	p. 122

The Reverend Samuel Kerrich (1736)
Oil painting on panel by Thomas Bardwell
By courtesy of Corpus Christi College, Cambridge

INTRODUCTION

Barbara Postlethwaite was born at Shotesham, Norfolk on 19th May 1707, the eldest child of the Reverend Mathew Postlethwaite and his wife Elizabeth Rogerson;[1] her sister Elizabeth followed a year later on 14th September 1708, and lastly their brother John in 1711. They were fortunate in having a father whose position in the clerical hierarchy was buttressed by marriage to the Bishop of Norwich's sister, and by receiving the living of Redenhall and promotion to Archdeacon of Norwich in 1742, while retaining the parish of Denton where the family had lived since 1714. Barbara's future husband, Samuel Kerrich, Vicar of Dersingham[2] numbered medical men, a brewer and clergy among his relations, to which (in common with Mathew Postlethwaite), was added the advantages of a Cambridge education.[3] Both men were fortunate in being able to enjoy that 'honorary gentleman status which was the prerogative of the more comfortably off clergy in Georgian England'.[4]

1. Mathew Postlethwaite (1679-1745), son of George and Elizabeth Postlethwaite of Bankside, Millum, Cumberland; educated St Paul's School, Corpus Christi and St John's Colleges, Cambridge. His uncle, John Postlethwaite, High Master of St Paul's was patron of Denton, to which his nephew was presented in 1714. Mathew Postlethwaite was later Rector of Redenhall and Archdeacon of Norwich, 1742. His first wife Elizabeth Rogerson, whom he married in 1704 died 29 March 1730. His second marriage to Matilda, sister of Thomas Gooch, later Bishop of Norwich took place in 1731. Mathew Postlethwaite was descended from the junior branch of a Cumberland landowning family: D.N.B. XVI, p. 205; C. Roy. Huddleston and R. S. Boumphrey, *Cumberland Families And Heraldry* (1978), p. 266.

2. Samuel Kerrich (1696-1768), eldest son of Thomas Kerrich 'druggist' of Harleston by Rebecca, second daughter of Samuel and Rebecca Kidman of Diss; educated St Paul's, Fellow of Corpus Christi College, Cambridge 1719-1729; D.D. 1735. Vicar of West Newton 1729-1731; Kerrich's acquaintance with Mathew Postlethwaite went back to his schooldays and was reinforced through their common regard for Kerrich's maternal uncle Charles Kidman. He married, first Jane Kitchingman in 1729, who died 22 August 1731, and secondly Barbara Postlethwaite in 1732: Venn III, p.10.; Hartshorne, pp. 37-38.

3. Another contemporary, Benjamin Rogers, Rector of Carleton, Bedfordshire, 1720-1771 has been described as a cleric of the 'middle grade'. He was not a pluralist, although he acted as Curate of Chellington from 1720 to 1761: Rogers was also married and had a family to support: C. D. Linnell (ed.), *The Diary of Benjamin Rogers, Rector of Carleton 1720-71* (Bedfordshire Historical Record Society XXX, Streatley, Beds. 1949), pp. viii - xiv.

4. The better-off clergy shared this status with lawyers, some doctors and dons: John Rule, *Albion's People: English Society 1714-1815* (1992), p. 48.

Barbara's marriage in 1732 led to the sisters' separation for nineteen years, as the living of Dersingham lay on the north western side of Norfolk.[5] Thereafter, meetings between them were somewhat infrequent, generally in the summer - the longest gap being from 1741 to 1744. But they wrote to each other sometimes twice weekly, such was their fondness for one another, and enough letters have survived for a picture to emerge of themselves, family and friends and perhaps a little of eighteenth century provincial society.

Family, Friends and Servants.

Barbara Kerrich's married life began in John Pell's old house, which despite repairs and improvements, was far from satisfactory, and always liable to flooding because of its situation.[6] In contrast, the rectory at Denton had been rebuilt 'with brick and covered with tile' in 1718.[7] Although eleven years younger than her husband, Barbara and Samuel Kerrich developed a close, tender relationship. In the early days of their marriage, Samuel Kerrich's remark to his wife that they 'generally chime[d] pretty well together', was confirmed by a friend observing them at King's Lynn some years later:

'Tis very easy for me to conceive you was nearer perfect happiness and true felicity in the enjoyment of the Dr's company and Miss, than Mrs Gregson was in partaking of all the diversions the mart could afford her'.[8]

But even this marriage had its darker side - in Barbara's case the loss of her first baby following several miscarriages:

5. Hartshorne, especially pp. 9-36.

6. *Ibid*, pp. 34, 62. The family moved to Dersingham Hall in 1753. In 1888 it became the property of Theodore Jannoch who was to become famous for his lilies of the valley and who held a warrant from King Edward VII and Queen Alexandra. It is now the Gamekeeper's Lodge Hotel: Simon Massen, *West Norfolk A Portrait in Old Picture Postcards* (West Drayton, Shropshire 1989), p. 51 and conversation with the author.

7. N(orfolk) R(ecord) O(ffice), DN/TER 53/3/10, 25 June 1735. The Rectory was extended c. 1839, and today is a private residence.

8. Ms 589, f. 166 28 April 1735; Ms 590, f. 46 Susanna Houghton to Barbara Kerrich, 26 March 1743.

The Old Hall Dersingham
From a postcard of c. 1906
Reproduced by kind permission of S.B.Publications

A View of the Church at Denton, Norfolk
Paul Sandby, pencil and watercolour
By courtesy of Agnew's, London

'..I can talk of nothing, nor think of nothing but the loss of my poor child which I had fixed my affections upon too soon. You'll wonder to hear me say it, but I believe if I hadn't the best of husbands it would almost break my heart, but he never leaves me, and is always contriving to divert me from my thoughts of it.'[9]

However, the birth of Tilly (Matilda) in 1742[10] and Thomas[11] six years later brought joy to both parents, and thereafter the doings of Tilly and her brother took up an increasing part of the correspondence, following Tilly from her weaning and first 'childish prattle' to her earliest efforts at walking and dancing, her dolls and games. At the age of three she was taken to Houghton and,

'was so merry and comical there, she made everybody laugh. She did run and fly about, and the housekeeper got her and laid her onto the velvet bed and kissed her, and was mightily pleased with her.'[12]

Four years later her interest was quickly aroused by a party of travelling actors:

'We have some good players come to Snettisham, and have been to see *The Beaux Strategem* , and *The Journey to London*. The entertainment after it was *The King and The Miller*, an exceeding good thing. I never saw it before, but Tilly entered into the plot so that she gave her papa a very good account of it, and put me in mind of several things that had escaped me.'[13]

Elizabeth frequently sent Tilly presents, taking a great interest in her niece's health and wellbeing. She applauded the child's interest in reading, noting her fondness for stories and encouraging her appetite

9. See below, pp.38-39

10. Matilda Kerrich (1742-1823), married half cousin Thomas Kerrich 5 Nov. 1767: Hartshorne, p. 64.

11. Thomas Kerrich (1748-1828), graduated Magdalene College, Cambridge 1771; followed by two and a half years on the Grand Tour; Principal Librarian of Cambridge University and Fellow of the Society of Antiquaries, 1797; Rector of Denton 1784-1828. His many surviving drawings, mainly of antiquarian subjects are an indication of wider artistic abilities: Andrew W. Moore, *Norfolk & The Grand Tour* (Ex. Catalogue, Norwich 1985), pp. 66-68; Hartshorne, p.66.

12. See below, p.61.

13. See below, p. 101

for riddles.[14] But Elizabeth's life as an unmarried daughter, suffering from poor health, was far from easy. She may well have been blessed with 'philosophical patience', but her letters are at times a litany of coughs, colds, colic, pains in the side and stomach, and on occasions, jaundice, swollen eyes and lameness. For long periods she stayed indoors, often confined to her room for weeks on end. Yet directly or indirectly she managed to keep a close eye on the goings on around her, however trivial:

'Miss Langley take a great deal of pains, I think, this hot weather, to hear Mr Baily preach. She walked to Starston after him in the morning, and to Redenhall in the afternoon'.[15]

And could be very judgemental:

'Miss Smith of Harleston and one of Mrs Pepit's daughters, an agreeable creature far beyond Miss Smith, came to see me'.[16]

Mathew Postlethwaite had remarried in 1730. His second wife was Matilda, sister of Thomas Gooch, Bishop of Norwich since 1738.[17] Elizabeth enjoyed a fairly good relationship with her stepmother, quizzically noting her hectic social round, but the atmosphere at the rectory was marred by her quarrelsome brother John, who returned home after a brief spell as a naval chaplain to sponge off his father, who repeatedly paid the young man's debts.[18] This strain on the family finances added to the difficulties of the Archdeacon's final years.

14. Her few surviving letters to Tilly in these early years show a gentle, teasing side to Elizabeth's character.

15. See below, p.15

16. See below, p. 98

17. Sir Thomas Gooch D.D. (1674-1754), Bishop of Norwich 1738-1748; Ely 1748-1754. Succeeded as 2nd Baronet on death of brother William in 1751. His portrait by Thomas Bardwell was included in the Benacre Hall Sale: G.E.C, V, pp.91-92; Sotheby's Catalogue, 9,10,11 May 2000 (lot 289).

18. John Postlethwaite was Chaplain to H.M.S. *Worcester* in 1738, having been educated at Merton College, Oxford: Hartshorne, p. 58. It seems that his sister Elizabeth sometimes took his part in family arguments: Ms 588, f. 141 Matilda Postlethwaite to Barbara Kerrich, 11 Dec. 1738.

6

The sisters remained close; they enjoyed exchanging gifts – plants and seeds for the garden, including hyacinths and lily of the valley roots, fish, meat and fruit. Dress materials and fashions were keenly discussed: the 'finery' worn by Miss Browne and Mr Folkes on their wedding day - 'the subject of all the tea tables hereabouts' - or the latest styles from London.[19] They shared a common interest in novels, Richardson's *Clarissa* causing Elizabeth to declare:

'...there is no reading of it without tears, indeed it have made me shed a great many. I never read anything so affecting and moving in my life'.[20]

'Cousin Johnson' their poor relation, makes an early appearance in the letters, at first a figure of fun but ultimately regarded with affection; she ran errands of all kinds between rectory and vicarage, and was a welcome source of news from Norwich.[21] Dr John Kerrich, was one of several Kerrich relatives who figured in their lives,[22] but the sisters were probably closest to the impecunious Charles Kerrich, surgeon and cleric,[23] who occasionally offered medical advice to both. Elizabeth faithfully reported the doings of Bunning Dalling and his family, including the extravagance that eventually led to the sale of their home.[24] The half-hearted courtship of Sukey Arrowsmith and the Reverend Robert Cremer, between August and October 1741, was anxiously encouraged by both sisters, but as Elizabeth saw, it was not to be:

19. See below, pp. 27, 80-82.
20. Ms 589, f. 97 Elizabeth Postlethwaite to Barbara Kerrich, 3 March 1749.
21. She was 'turned out of house and home' in October 1735. The Postlethwaites acted quickly to set her up 'for a small trader', over against St Peter's Church near the White Swan in Norwich: Ms 588, f. 125 Matilda Postlethwaite to Barbara Kerrich, 14 Oct. 1735; Ms 591, f. 83 Mathew Postlethwaite to Samuel Kerrich, 17 Nov. 1735.
22. John Kerrich M.D. (1693-1762), uncle of Samuel Kerrich, son of Walter Kerrich 'brewer' of Harleston and Ann Dove; married Mary, daughter of Simon Patrick. Practised physic at Bury St. Edmunds: Venn III, p.10.
23. Charles Kerrich, younger brother of the Reverend Samuel Kerrich, studied medicine in London; took orders and became Rector of Kenninghall in 1749, but continued to practise medicine at Harleston: Hartshorne, pp. 21-22.
24. See below, p. 67.

'Miss Sukey Arrowsmith's match is quite off. Her gentleman have not used her handsomely. He wouldn't settle any part of his estate upon her. If she would have him without any security he would marry her, but not else. She says she thinks she is born not to be married'.[25]

Servants and the problems they caused were another mutual topic, more so as both families shared the labours of the Brady girls, originally from Denton, daughters of Goodman Brady one of Mathew Postlethwaite's parishioners. They would not always work with other servants, and at least one, Sukey, was accused of 'deception', and another, Ruth, was feared for her 'bad temper'.[26] In contrast, Sarah, Barbara Kerrich's wet nurse came to be regarded almost as a member of the family, and there was great sadness at her death in childbirth.[27]

At this period deep religious conviction was not that important in a parson's wife (or daughter), although a basic commitment to religious duty was expected. From the evidence of the letters, both sisters had a conventional approach to Christianity[28] and as little questioning of doctrine as they had for their father's whig politics.[29] But this did not exclude an interest in the workings of ecclesiastical patronage, or local disputes between parsons and members of their congregations.[30] They were very relieved when their brother John succeeded his father at Denton, and for a while Elizabeth stayed on as his housekeeper, an increasingly uncomfortable situation only ending

25. See below, p. 49.. According to Matilda Postlethwaite she had already been rejected by another suitor 'Mr Schuldam' of Bungay on similar grounds: Ms 588, f. 160 Matilda Postlethwaite to Barbara Kerrich, 28 March 1741.

26. There were four of them: Tabby, Ruth, Sukey, Mary and Betty.

27. See below, p. 85.

28. Jane Austen, herself a clergyman's daughter, seldom mentioned religion in her early adult life, except when writing letters of condolence to bereaved relations. It plays an equally minor role in this correspondence: Irene Collins, *Jane Austen and the Clergy* (1994), p. 125.

29. Nor was this so unusual, for the correspondence of their contemporaries, the Oxfordshire Squire, Henry Purefoy and his mother Elizabeth are also marked by 'a complete absence of any allusions to politics': G. Eland (ed.), *Purefoy Letters 1735-1753* (2v., 1931), I, pp. xxi, 202.

30. See below, pp. 54-55, 73.

at his death in a riding accident in 1750. She helped wind up her brother's estate,[31] and moved, first to Norwich and then to Dersingham to join her sister. It seems fitting that both sisters were buried in the chancel of St Nicholas's church, where their memorials can be seen today.[32]

Parish and Neighbourhood

'You must get as much company as you can to you and make all the little visits in the parish and the neighbourhood that you can make without fatiguing yourself'

Samuel Kerrich urged his young wife during one of his periodical absences in Cambridge.[33] This was good advice at a time when the parson and his family often found themselves socially isolated in small rural communities, many with less than 500 inhabitants[34], with no immediate neighbours of comparable standing, and where his wife's public duties were not over burdensome (although the management of a household was rarely altogether free from anxieties).[35] Fortunately, the patron of the living, Colonel James Hoste, lived at Sandringham, less than a mile away. Moreover, his son[36] had been a pupil of Samuel

31. See below pp. 109,110 and Appendix I, pp. 123-125.

32. On Barbara's death in 1762, Elizabeth joined her niece Tilly at Burnham Market, dying there in 1794: Hartshorne, pp. 64 - 66.

33. Ms 589, f. 162 13 April 1735.

34. In 1801 four fifths of the population of England still lived in rural parishes. A clerical survey showed the majority of the 10,500 parishes had fewer than 500 inhabitants, 3,000 fewer than 200, and 960 less than 100. The population of Denton in 1801 was 451, Dersingham, 457: I.Collins, op. cit, p. 92; *The Clerical Guide or Ecclesiastical Directory* (1817), p. 54.

35. Apart from her religious duties, a parson's wife normally presided over her household, which meant taking an active role in the dairy and garden. She was also generally expected to distribute charitable gifts, might prepare medicines for the poor and go sick-visiting. Mathew Postlethwaite briefly alluded to his daughters distributing money to the Denton poor at Christmas time: Collins, p. 125; Ms 591, f. 45 Mathew Postlethwaite to Samuel Kerrich, 15 Dec. 1732.

36. James Hoste (1705-1744), M.P. Bramber, Sussex 1728-1734, married Susan, daughter of Anthony Hammond of South Wootton, Norfolk. His father's first wife, Elizabeth Walpole, was Sir Robert Walpole's aunt: Sedgwick, II, p. 151.

Kerrich's at Cambridge and relations between the two families were good.[37] Gifts of game and fish were gratefully recorded in Barbara's letters, together with frequent invitations to dinner, while the Hostes were the happy recipients of newspapers from the vicarage. Much of the land in the parish, including the rather dilapidated house lived in by the Kerriches, was part of the Pell estate bought by Colonel Walpole in 1697 and inherited by his son Sir Robert Walpole.[38] The Hoste and Walpole families were related by marriage (if not always on good terms), so that one way or another, Samuel and Barbara Kerrich had links with the most powerful families within the county, and beyond. Hence the scraps of political gossip to be found in the letters, most notably Lord Townshend's reflections on his enforced retirement to Raynham, and the more personal dealings of Barbara Kerrich with the inhabitants of Houghton.[39]

Other neighbours making frequent appearances in her letters include the Cremers - the Reverend Robert Cremer, Rector of Brancaster[40] and his sister, proudly described by Barbara as 'very pretty company' and her 'best friend', and a few years later another clerical couple, the Gregsons at Little Massingham.[41] All these lived close at hand, but when their company palled, there were the attractions of King's Lynn less than ten miles from Dersingham, a bustling port with its market and shops, and further acquaintances including 'Recorder Berney'[42] and the Browne family, Dr Browne, a wealthy physician, his wife and daughter.[43]

Denton and the nearby rural parishes of Topcroft and Starston were the homes of various friends and acquaintances of the Postlethwaites, including Bunning Dalling[44] in Denton itself, the

37. Hartshorne, p.20.

38. J.H. Plumb, *Sir Robert Walpole: The Making of a Statesman* (1956), p.85.

39. See below, pp. 20, 101.

40 Robert Cremer (1683-1751), Vicar of Babingley and Sandringham 1713, Rector of Brancaster 1716-1751: Foster (Early Series), I, p. 348; Ms 591, f. 186 Barbara Kerrich to Samuel Kerrich, 29 Oct. 1732.

41. Thomas Gregson (born 1681), Rector of Little Massingham 1715 and of Rougham 1723: Foster (Early Series), II, p. 604.

42. Thomas Berney (1685-1745), Recorder of King's Lynn 1730-1745. Matilda Postlethwaite complained of his family's dullness: Venn,I, p.142; Ms 588, f.155 Matilda Postlethwaite to Barbara Kerrich, July. 1740.

43. William Browne M.D. (1692-1774), Practised medicine at King's Lynn before moving to London:Venn, I, p. 240.

44. Bunning Dalling (fl. 1722-1748), 'of Fritton, Gent' :NRO PD136/4 Denton Parish Register 1715-1812.

Arrowsmiths at Starston[45] and the Smith family at Topcroft.[46] Bungay lay close by, but it was to Harleston that the Postlethwaites looked for diversions. Both sisters were invited to Harleston Fair by their friend Isabella Barry:[47]

'After three weeks consideration, I have at last determined to be at Harleston Fair, where I hope to have the favour of meeting you and Miss Betty: and that you would engage all the company you can that we may have a good raffle'.[48]

The midsummer fair began on 24th June. There were theatricals too, at the Swan Inn:[49]

'The players have come to Harleston, they have a great deal of company. They have taken some nights 15 or 16 pound'.[50].

On this particular occasion Elizabeth's stepmother had gone to the play with a party that included 'Mrs Harman, Mrs Buxton, Lady Bacon and the Misses Arrowsmiths'. Bungay assembly rooms lacked the popularity of Ditchingham's, where cards, particularly quadrille were the main attraction, drawing 'a great deal of good company'.[51]

45. Thomas Arrowsmith (1674-1729), Rector of Starston and Alburgh 1699-1729; married Elizabeth, daughter of John Smith of Cratfield, Suffolk: Foster (Early Series), I p. 32; Blomefield, V, p. 350.

46. There were branches of the Smith family at Topcroft and Harleston: Blomefield, V, p.408.

47 Isabella Barry who shared Barbara Kerrich's musical interests was the daughter of Lambe Barry (1706-1768) of Syleham, Suffolk. He was made High Sheriff of Suffolk in 1748 and c.1750 Gainsborough painted his portrait: Venn I, p. 98; Sir Ellis Waterhouse, *Gainsborough* (1958), No. 40.

48. Ms 590, f. 13 Isabella Barry to Barbara Kerrich, 22 June 1729.

49 There were two annual fairs at Harleston and a weekly market. The room at the Swan Inn was in use for balls by 1732: Blomefield, V, p. 356; Peter Borsay, *The English Urban Renaissance: Culture and Society in the Provincial Town 1660-1770* (Oxford 1989), App.5, p. 340.

50. See below, p. 24.

51. Ms 588, f. 139 Matilda Postlethwaite to Barbara Kerrich, 30 Nov. 1738.

Elizabeth's poor health forced her to observe such activities mostly at a distance, but fortunately she was sometimes able to take part in receiving visitors, a major feature of the social round at both Denton and Dersingham. As her stepmother was the Bishop's sister these were often rather grand occasions. 'The Houghtons, the Dean and his lady, and Miss Betty and four servants' were entertained in August 1738 and at another time 'Dr Gooch and lady and little master and three servants' were expected to stay 'about a fortnight'.[52] Such visits made considerable demands on their hosts. When the Bishop came in October 1739, the menu at dinner included 'a brace of hare, 15 pigeons, a lease of pheasants, two brace of partridges, a brace of woodcock, a couple of wilds duck and a couple of teal'.[53] Fortunately there was less formality with friends such as Sukey Arrowsmith, or when Barbara arrived. Perhaps card-playing was their most popular activity, especially in winter; it was something Elizabeth greatly enjoyed:

> 'My sister, Miss Betty and I play at ombre from dinner till supper and I assure you Miss Betty is a dab at it. She beats her teacher, and my brother is courageous, gaming so much.' [54]

There was also music, with Barbara singing and playing on the spinet. In the summer there was the garden to enjoy, fondly recalled years later by Susanna Houghton, when she wrote of 'the pleasant walks and the happy days' at Denton.[55]

Conclusion

Both sisters went to school, Barbara first at Norwich, where she met her friend Isabella Barry, then later with Elizabeth to 'Mrs Wetherel's, Bury St Edmunds, where the curriculum would have consisted of reading, writing, music and dancing, as well as 'curious work' such as embroidery, needlework, shell-work and japanning, then regarded as

52. Ms 588, f. 124 as above, 8 Aug. 1735; see below, p.31.
53. Ms 588, f. 145 as above, 30 Oct. 1739.
54. Ms 589, f. 239 Elizabeth Townshend to Barbara Kerrich, - Jan. 1739.
55. Ms 590, f. 58 Susanna Houghton to Barbara Kerrich, n.d.

the sort of education to equip a girl from the middle class.[56] Perhaps Mrs Wetherel taught them to write in that breathless style which makes much of their correspondence so endearing. 'A letter,' grumbled Evelyn Waugh to his long-suffering wife Laura, 'should be a form of conversation; write as though you are talking to me.' This conversational quality, the hallmark of letter-writing at its best, helps to bring the sisters to life, revealing a clear portrait of both, as well as something of the age in which they lived, its expansive qualities as well as its harshness.[57]

They made no attempt to conceal the bleaker aspects of eighteenth century life - death in childbirth, infant mortality, and above all the scourge of smallpox which had no respect for age, sex or class. In contrast there is plenty of evidence of its social activities, the entertaining and visiting that were so pleasant a feature of country life at this time, together with examples of the widespread interest in music, literature and drama, often centred on assembly rooms and inns, to be found in all but the smallest of provincial towns. Growing national prosperity helped to finance an increasing demand for all kinds of consumer goods, whilst providing ample leisure for small but expanding numbers of people to enjoy them. Developments in science and technology, improvements in farming and communications were slowly beginning to transform the country in economic and social terms. Some, but not all, of these trends are apparent in the letters and some were clearer to contemporaries than others.[58] Subtler changes in the relationships between men and women were also taking place, notably the emergence of what has been called 'the companionate marriage', together with less formal, more affectionate

56. Both may well have been boarding schools (Mrs Wetherel's certainly was), popular from the late seventeenth century onwards, although it was not uncommon for girls to be educated at home: Hartshorne, p. 34 and below, p. 17; Lawrence Stone, *The Family, Sex and Marriage in England 1500-1800* (Harmondsworth, Middlesex 1979), p. 230.

57. Mark. Amory (ed.), *The Letters of Evelyn Waugh* (1980), Evelyn Waugh to Laura Waugh 7 Jan. 1945, p. 195; Eva Figes says of letter writing: 'It involves self-expression, that is, a willingness to express what one is, and does, and thinks as though ink and paper were no barrier, but as open as the atmosphere which carries our voices when we speak.' Eva Figes, *Women's Letters in Wartime 1450-1945* (1993), p. 9.

58. On medicine, see Roy Porter, *Disease, medicine and society in England, 1550-1860* (Cambridge 1993); on urban culture and society, P. Borsay, op. cit.; on leisure and consumerism, Neil McKendrick, John. Brewer and J. H. Plumb (eds.), *The Birth of a Consumer Society: The Commercialization of Eighteenth Century England* (1983).

attitudes of parents towards their children.[59] If Barbara and Samuel Kerrich seem to offer a good example of these developments some of their friends and acquaintances were not so fortunate. It was reported that when Mrs Artis was seriously ill her husband[60] behaved as though 'his whole task is of getting another wife [he] shows no manner of concern for this', while Justice Kerrich's indecent haste to seek out a successor on the death of his second wife, was a cause for comment: and Mr Farrow was reputed to beat his wife and keep her short of money.[61] Nor were the provision of a dowry or settlement any guarantee of security or satisfaction in marriage, as Sukey Arrowsmith's experience demonstrates.[62] Thus for many, life continued to follow more traditional paths in relationships as in other respects.

A Carrier's Cart outside a Country Inn
From a print c.1800

59. L. Stone, op. cit., pp. 217-224; 254-267; Anne Laurence, *Women In England 1500-1760: A Social History* (1996), especially pp. 56-60 and 89-92 .For a recent more critical discussion of Stone's views, see Amanda Vickery, *The Gentleman's Daughter: Women's Lives in Georgian England* (New Haven U.S.A and London 1998), notably the introduction, pp. 1-12 and Ch. 2 pp. 39-86.

60. Lane Artis Esq. of Yarmouth: Ms 588 f. 117, 23 June.

61. Ms 588 f. 128, Matilda Postlethwaite to Barbara Kerrich, 25 June 1736; f.152, 20 June 1740; f. 189, 6 May 1743.

62. See below, pp. 64-65 and notes 81 and 88.

~~~~~~

THE TEXT

~~~~~~

Few letters have survived for the years 1733 to 1740. All 38 of Barbara Kerrich's are published and 64 of Elizabeth Postlethwaite's 107. Their correspondence began on 27 May 1733[1], six months after Barbara's wedding. Now read on...

From Elizabeth Postlethwaite
Denton 27 May, 1733

Dear Sister,

We this morning received your letter dated the 6 of May and would have answered your last letter sooner, but my father and mother both of them wrote and then I waited for Mr Burgess coming. He set out tomorrow morning so that we can't get the tea which you desired, but my mother have half a pound in the house that she will let you have. Mr Brock[2] come soon and I will get him to bring it for you. My father see my uncle when he was at London and he was wonderfully civil and he sent my mother a present of green tea and me of chocolate.

My father bought a pair of very fine coach horses when he was there and one of them was taken ill in the coming home, so were obliged to leave him upon the road. Ammi went last Thursday to have fetched him home, but he was not fit to come, nor will not be this fortnight or 3 weeks, and they never have been roaded yet.

Mrs Dalling says she can't come this Summer, I did desire to have come this month but now it will be uncertain when can I find by my brother's letter to Mr Charles Kerrich you are not got perfectly well yet, which makes it the more uneasy to me till I can see you. I have still returns of old cough. Give my service to Miss Raye[3] and tell her if

---

1. Possibly earlier, according to note by Albert Hartshorne.
2. Roger Brock senior acted as a messenger between Denton and Dersingham. His namesake, the younger Roger Brock is first mentioned in 1743 as one of Samuel Kerrich's tenants: Ms 591, f. 139, 3 Feb. 1743, f. 132, 1 Jan. 1743.
3. Rebecca Raye, sister of Charles Raye kept house at Dersingham for Samuel and Barbara Kerrich, prior to them living there: Hartshorne, pp. 202, 207.

I do come through Diss I will let her father know it. Dr Kerrich and his lady have been at Harleston and came to see us before they went away. If is Sarah grows so fat, I am feared you must get your trifling parlour enlarged. I have heard nothing of her father and mother. Tell Tabby her father is very well, which I hope will comfort her under losses.

We were a fishing at Mr Dalling's last Friday. He is very merry and send his service, and will make a box for your tobacco ashes that you may keep your teeth clean. I would have you buy me one of those hats against I come. My mother would have answer letter by Mr Burgess if she had time. My pen is so bad and I have made so many blunders I don't believe you can read it You must send the canister back.

From Elizabeth Postlethwaite
Denton, 18 June 1733

Dear Sister,

I have sent you the pound of Bohea tea by Mr Brock. I did not know but you might want it before I can come, for this warm weather do not agree so well with me as I was in hopes it would. It makes me faint and I have often returns of my cough. I am to try the Bath[4] again when our horses are fit, and till then I am to go into a tub of water. I hope with that and the bark[5] I shall be able to see Dersingham before Summer be gone. I can give a very little account of our neighbours, for we have had hardly any to see us but Mr Barry's family; they were here last Thursday, Mrs Barry came with them.

Miss Langley take a great deal of pains, I think, this hot weather, to hear Mr Baily preach. She walked to Starston after him in the morning, and to Redenhall in the afternoon. Mr Dalling give his service and have sent you a fine large substantial box, there is one place to lay your brush. I have not seen Miss Sukey nor don't expect it. You dropped the letter Mrs Arrowsmith wrote you in the cellar and my mother found it, and she was very angry with her for writing in that manner, and answered, but Mrs Arrowsmith have not taken any notice of it yet.

4. Bath, the spa.
5. Jesuit's bark (or Peruvian bark), the basis of quinine was an effective remedy against malaria then known as 'the ague', widespread in low-lying areas of England: R. Porter, op. cit., p. 8.

Major Houghton[6] and his lady came the other day just as we were going to dinner. She said she asked Mr Kidman after you. He told her you were big with child, very near your time. I have this minute received a letter from my brother, he tell me he is at Mr Wallis's[7] and intend after the act to see you. I desire you would send my hat. If I get well enough to come I shall want it to come in.

From Barbara Kerrich
Dersingham, 21 June 1733

Dear Sister,

I am very much concerned to hear your cough is no better yet, I pray God the Bath may do you more good than it did last year. I hope you will try it no longer than you find it agrees with you. I shall write to know every day how you go on, for I think it an age since I saw you.

I have sent your hat. I suppose you have seen of them before this time, some people here wear them a little turned up of each side as old women do, and smaller than this, but I think this size most useful. I wish it had been finer, but I could get no better at Lynn. I am sadly vexed I should be so careless of Mrs Arrowsmith's letter because it may make a great uneasiness, though I wonder my mother should take notice of it considering all things, but in the meantime Mrs Arrowsmith must think me very tardy when I profess so much friendship for Miss Sukey.

I suppose my uncle Kidman[8] dreamt I was big with child and so forgot how he heard it. I thank God I am very well now, and I think that better than being with child. Give my service to Mr Dalling and thanks for the bountiful strong box he send me and tell him I wish he had sent it full of Denton wood ashes, to make lye[9] with to white my sheets. I have bought two pair of Mr Brock for our own bed. Pray let me hear from you very often, I don't grudge paying for your letters.

6. John Houghton (fl. 1720-1762) of Bramerton: Venn, II, p.413.

7. The interest of John Wallis was unsuccessfully sought by Mathew Postlethwaite with a view to obtaining a Fellowship at Magdalen College, Oxford for his son, John. The young man was invited by Wallis to his home at Eversley, Hampshire: Ms 587, f. 307 John Wallis to Mathew Postlethwaite, April 1734.

8. Charles Kidman (fl. 1663-1740) Fellow of Corpus Christi College, Cambridge 1685-1710. Chaplain to Archbishop Tenison; Rector of Grantchester Cambs., 1703-1737; Rector of Banham till 1735; Rector of Thwaite, Suffolk 1722-1740: Venn III, p. 15.

9. 'A composition of ashes and water to wash and scour withal.' Bailey

P.S I hear Ammi[10] is as good at bleeding of calves as he is at stealing and making of mischief.

One of our old school fellows is coming to see me at midsummer, Miss Greenwood that boarded at Mrs Wetherel's at Bury. She lives at Downham and Mrs Sharp was there a little while ago. She said she was mightily pleased to hear of me. Miss Greenwood has happened of a most sad misfortune. She was lamed with bleeding and her arm is quite withered now, how long it has been done I don't know, but 'tis thought it must be her death, and she is very cheerful and easy under it.

From Elizabeth Postlethwaite
Denton, 13 July 1733

Dear Sister,

We were yesterday at Mr Smith's[11] of Topcroft, which have tired me so much that I am hardly fit to write, but you being desirous of hearing often how I am and how bathing agrees with me, which I hope in time will do me service of strengthening those parts which are so much weakened by my cough, I am in hopes the humour is pretty well carried off at present. Change of weather do not affect so much as it used to do. Anything of exercise make me cough, the motion of the coach in rough roads I can't bear, but I go only into a tub of water about three times a week. Mrs Smith have lately buried her mother Mrs Churchman. She lay ill but a week, her daughters did not know it till she was dead and buried. She desired they might not.

Sir Robert Walpole[12] lay at Sir Charles Turner's[13] on Monday night and dined there on the Tuesday. Sir Charles invited some of the

10. Ammi had been charged with defaming the wife of 'Mr Barnes': Ms 591, f. 53, 6 Sept. 1734. Elisha Barnes, widower of Alburgh, married Mary Gowing of Denton 16 April 1734: NRO PD 136/4.

11. George Smith married Mary, third daughter of William Churchman Esq. of Illington. Smith was Sheriff of Norfolk in 1735 and died in December 1745: Blomefield, V, p. 407-408.

12. Sir Robert Walpole, Ist Earl of Orford (1676-1745), M.P. King's Lynn 1702-1712, 1713-1742; Prime Minister and Chancellor of the Exchequer 1715-1717, 1721-1742. Re-built Houghton, the family seat from 1721 onwards: Harvey, p. 869.

13. Sir Charles Turner, Ist Baronet (1666-1738), M.P. King's Lynn 1695-1728; a Lord of the Treasury 1720-1730. He was a close friend of Walpole's: Sedgwick, II, pp. 486-487.

neighbouring gentlemen, and my father was one, and from thence they went to Norwich where my father see Major Hoste. He told him that you and my brother were mighty well.

Miss Peggy Bransby is married, they talk of going to live at London and to board with Mr Goldson. Mr Newgate and his wife this afternoon come to make a visit, which prevent my writing any more at present, only desiring you to let me hear from you all opportunities you have, which I must content myself with till I be able to come. Pray tell Sarah I see her mother as we came from Topcroft, but were so soon past could not speak to her, but she looks as if she were well. Remember me to Tabby.

From Elizabeth Postlethwaite
Denton, 9 August 1733

Dear Sister,

I take this opportunity of writing and sending your cloak by Mr Raye,[14] for I shan't be fit to undertake so long a journey as to Dersingham this Summer, for those visits I have gone, tired and wearied me so much that I always coughed the next morning. My father met Sir Benjamin[15] at the Dean's this week. He says he have thought of something that he is in hopes will be of great service to me.

Mrs Arrowsmith called here the other day as she was going to Starston and invited my mother very earnestly to go and see her, so that I believe they will be very good friends again now. Mrs Smith[16] of Harleston is disappointed of her journey for she was taken very ill of a fever a day or two before she should have gone. Mrs Townshend[17] is gone to Cambridge to be with Mrs Gooch the time of her lying in, and then Mrs Artis and she talks of going to Bath.

14. Charles Raye (fl. 1727-1754), first cousin of Samuel Kerrich; Minor Canon of Norwich, Vicar of Calthorpe and Thwaite 1734-1739; Chaplain to the Bishop of Ely 1740-1743 and Vicar of St Peter's, St Albans, Herts. 1743-1754: Venn, III, p. 427; Hartshorne p. 207.

15. Sir Benjamin Wrench M.D. (1666-1747), 'a distinguished physician in Norwich for many years': Ms 588, f. 109 Mathew Postlethwaite to Barbara Kerrich, 9 Feb. 1737; Venn, IV, p. 470.

16. Bransby Bransby, married Offley Smith Esq, of Harleston, younger son of George Smith and Mary Churchman: Blomefield, V, p. 408.

17. Elizabeth Townshend (fl. 1703-1746) daughter of William Sherlock, Dean of St Paul's, sister of Bishop Gooch's first wife, Mary, and widow of Horatio Townshend(?) (c.1679-1706), Rector of Tacolneston: Hartshorne, p.44; Venn, IV, p. 259.

On Sunday last we had a very bad tempest here and were very much frightened with it, for my father had the misfortune to have one of the barns that belong to Baldry's Farm burnt down to the ground with it that which stood by the house where Everard lived.

You have said nothing about Tabby a long time, I want to hear how she goes on. Her father often ask whether she be a good girl. Tell my brother I would have him come home, for I want his company. I wish you would contrive to come with him, if you don't I am afraid I shan't see you till next Spring. All your neighbours ask after you and send their service, and hope to see you when you come to Denton again.

From Barbara Kerrich
Dersingham 29 October 1733

Dear Sister,

I am very much pleased to hear you have done with the mercury[18] for everybody that I have heard speak of it, say it is very lucky for them that take it if they find no hurt from it, but I wanted to have you read one of the papers in the magazine for August (I think it was), 'tis a comical piece of work they make of it there. As for the ladies, he says, he does not see how it can possibly do them any good unless it should turn 'em into barometers, that they may know whether it will be proper to go a visiting and when to be in bed, if you have not read it, pray do.[19]

Now you'll expect I should say something about my doctor: he is very slow and goes by degrees from one thing to another; and I hope my cure will be the more lasting and not return as it used to do. I believe he is very safe and has good judgement. He is not for much physic, but has forbid me meat suppers wholly, which I dare say has done me good.

18. Mercury treatment was held to be very dangerous: Buchan, pp. 295, 405, 406n. Elizabeth probably had scurvy. A fellow sufferer, Sarah, Duchess of Marlborough went to Scarborough spa in search of relief from the complaint, writing to her grand-daughter Diana, Duchess of Bedford on 21 July 1732: 'I have taken these waters but seven days and the itching that tormented me so much, which was from the scurvy is almost gone'. Gladys Scott Thomson, *Letters of a Grandmother 1732-1735* (1944), pp. 31, 53.

19. 'And it is to be hoped, that with proper observation, every lady that takes it, will become a barometer, and foretell the weather by the rise and fall of the quicksilver in her guts, as well as any weatherglass whatever': G.M. III (1733), p. 418.

Doctor Kerrich told me you were not come from Mr Barry's yet, but I suppose you will by that time these letters get to Denton. Mr Kerrich[20] went with the gentlemen to Raynham, and Lord Townshend[21] insisted upon their dining and supping with him and put me into a very great fright, for just as I was expecting them home, there was a messenger sent on purpose to me from Raynham, with a letter from Mr Kerrich to tell me they must stay all night. They were extremely courteously and handsomely received by my Lord. They say he seems a mighty happy man quite free from all the troubles of the great ones and spends his time in planting and improving his own seat. Mr Patrick and the Dr were very well pleased with that and Houghton too.

I must tell you how civil they have been at Sandringham, especially since I have been ill. They sent me a nice little sucking pig, and then the Major brought me a brace of partridges and three or four woodcocks his own self, because he heard I loved them. I was surprised to hear of Mrs Custance's death, though I think her life was not happy enough to make her desire it long. Let me hear from you as soon as you can.

P.S. Duty to my father and mother. You need not have mentioned the money my brother borrowed here, for you know we owe you more.

From Elizabeth Postlethwaite
Denton, 28 December 1733

Dear Sister,

I have designed writing to you a long time but have always been prevented by one thing or other. My father received Mr Kerrich's letter, where he says you talk of coming in the Spring. I shall think the time long till it come, for it's a prodigious while since I see you. I thank God I hold pretty well at present. I design to nurse and take a great deal of care of myself this Winter, that I may be able to go back with you.

20. Samuel Kerrich did not become a doctor of divinity until 1735, and thereafter is invariably referred to as 'the Dr'.

21. Charles Townshend, 2nd Viscount Townshend (1674-1738), Secretary of State for the Northern Department 1714-1716, 1721-1730; Lord Lieutenant of Norfolk 1701-1713, 1714-1730. He retired from political life in 1730 following serious disagreements with Walpole, devoting himself thereafter to his estate at Raynham: D.N.B. XIX, pp. 1036-1043.

Raynham Hall, Norfolk, seat of Lord Townshend (1779)
Drawn and engraved by William Watts
By courtesy of the Witt Library, Courtauld Institute, London

A Fishing Party
Oil painting by
William Hogarth
By permission of the
Trustees of Dulwich
Picture Gallery

We go out nowhere and have but very little company come, so that I have no news to tell you only that Mr John Buxton's[22] daughter is a going to marry, but I don't know to who, but they say it's a good match for her. She was here last night, I think she look worse than ever. She came with her sister Taylor who asked for you. She is very merry, and I thought very well dressed for riding, but she made a great many excuses. My father[23] will take care to send Barnes's rent by Mr Brock, he talks of coming soon.

I have sent you a song which is supposed to be made by Dr Paston[24] or Mr Smith, but I must conclude or I shan't have room to write it. I shall be glad to hear you are got perfectly well

The Harleston Cavalcade

'Come listen good folks I will tell you a tale
Of the noble exploits of a brewer of ale,
With five or six fools that followed his tail,
Which none of 'em can deny.

This man to show his great zeal for the cause
Got a parcel of puppies to spread out their paws,
And Black Jack and Black Charles to open their jaws,
Which none of 'em can deny.

To the Town he came with a mob at his arse,
To see how they looked was a very good farce,
For Bacon and Wodehouse they hardly could pass,
Which none of 'em can deny.

22. John Buxton (1685-1731), amateur architect of Tibenham and Shadwell Lodge employed Thomas Bardwell to decorate the hall at Shadwell in 1728. Several members of his family subsequently had their portraits painted by Bardwell, as did Elizabeth Postlethwaite and Barbara Kerrich: M. Kirby Talley, 'Thomas Bardwell of Bungay, Artist and Author 1704–1767', *Walpole Society* 46 (Oxford 1976-1978), pp. 95, 132-134, and Appendix 2 below p.125-126.

23. Mathew Postlethwaite usually passed on matters relating to his son-in-law's tenants in the parishes of Denton and Alburgh. A map of 1752 shows Samuel Kerrich as owner of c.144 acres in Denton, sharing the ownership of c.45 others with Elizabeth Postlethwaite. In addition he had c.23 in Alburgh.: NRO MC 1744/1. In 1734 Kerrich was the proprietor of the King's Head, Bungay, 'in the tenure of Mary Knight, widow': Guildhall Library, London, Ms 11936/38 Sun Fire Insurance Policy Registers Old Series 10, 1733-34 No. 63306, 22 March 1734.

24. James Paston M.D.(1675-1752) who practised at Harleston: Venn, III, p.317.

With trumpets and fiddles they entered the town,
With turd coloured ribbands and many clown,
But few of 'em had votes as to all men is know,
Which none of 'em can deny.

There's vice Chamberlain Coke just come to an estate,
And Morden who hopes in time to be great,
If in the Parliament house he can get a seat,
Which none of 'em can deny...'[25]

From Elizabeth Postlethwaite
Denton, 28 February 1734

Dear Sister,

I had a mind to write to let you know that I have recovered the disorder the pills gave me, and I have not coughed since, but find myself faint and very tender that I dare not venture out of my chamber yet, but hope as the Spring come on and the weather warmer it will recover my strength.

Mrs Townshend went to Yarmouth last Tuesday, but Mrs Artis and she can't agree no longer, so she talk of coming to Denton again soon to live wholly here, but I wish she may get a husband before I see her again. I believe she would like it very well, she talked of a gentleman that admire her. She have bought a very handsome night gown[26] of a rich brocaded silk with all colours and suit of linen of a Brussels lace, so I hope all together will tempt him.

Justice Kerrich's[27] match go on a great pace with Miss Mary Baron. Miss Barry was here this week and tell me they talk at Harleston as if it would not be long before he brought her home. My

---

25. This song anticipates the violent partisan struggle that marked the general election of 1734. At Norfolk's county contest the Tory candidates Sir Edmund Bacon Bart and William Wodehouse defeated their Whig op'ponents William Morden and Robert Coke by a mere six votes: Sedgwick, I, p. 289.

26 A gown for evening wear. For a more detailed discussion of female fashion amongst the gentry see Anne Buck, *Dress in Eighteenth Century England* (1979), pp. 64-103.

27 Simon Kerrich J.P (1697-1748) younger brother of John Kerrich M.D. Simon Kerrich married secondly, Mary, youngest daughter of John Baron Dean of Norwich 1732-1739. She died 13 May 1740: NRO MC 1578/1 Miscellaneous papers, n.p; Venn, I, p. 95.

cousin Johnson desire to know whether you sent the quilted coat which you promised her by the coach that carried you home, if you did it's lost. I am quite tired or else I could have said more. I wish myself with you every day.

From Elizabeth Postlethwaite
Denton, 13 July 1734

Dear Sister,

I have sent you by Mr Brock your gloves and some pink seed,[28] and next time he come he is to bring the tansy,[29] for this is not a right time of the year to take it up.

My mother was to see Mrs Arrowsmith last week and invited Miss Sukey and her sister to stay with me. Miss Sukey[30] want very much to come to Dersingham. I believe she had a good mind to have come now with Mr Brock if she had things with her that were fit for the journey. The players are come to Harleston, they have a great deal of company. They have taken some nights 15 or 16 pound. Mrs Hannah Buxton sent to my mother yesterday morning to meet her there at night and Lady Bacon is come to Mr Sayer's[31] so my mother went to return her visit, and Miss Arrowsmith's with her, and from thence they went to the play. I wish we may have good luck with your eggs for we were forced to send them to Mrs Dalling's, we haven't one hen that will set. I can fix no time yet for coming for I have not been quite so well as when you were here, I have had two or three fits of coughing. I found your pocketbook and have sent the receipt.

P.S. Half a pound of flour, half a pound of sugar, a quarter pound of butter, three eggs, two spoonfuls of sack. Rub the butter and flour very

28. Perhaps carnations, sweet williams or stocks, all widely grown in borders and knots: Elizabeth Banks, *Creating Period Gardens*, (Oxford 1991), pp. 208, 210.

29. Served as a flavouring for puddings, and was held to relieve 'griping pains of the bowels' and pains in the joints: Culpeper's *Complete Herbal* (n.d.), pp. 361, 362.

30. She had been eager to make the journey since April, but 'wants a convenient vehicle or a pair of wings…, till which time she must remain where she is, for a horse she can't manage it discompose her garments and show her legs and make her breech sore and many complaints': Ms 588, f.122 Matilda Postlethwaite to Barbara Kerrich, April 1734.

31. Thomas Sayer, Gent. of Pulham, married Muriel, daughter of Richard Browne of Sparkes in Tacolneston: Blomefield, V, p. 401.

The Swan at Harleston
Photograph c. 1900
By courtesy of the Norfolk Studies Library

well together, then put the sugar to it and after the eggs and wine are well beaten, mix all together just before they go into the oven. My mother wrote to you about a fortnight ago.

From Barbara Kerrich
Dersingham, 10 March 1735

Dear Sister,

I am mighty glad to hear from you by your own hand, because it gives me a double assurance of your being better, but I am afraid not well enough for me to ask your coming hither in April when Mr Kerrich goes to Cambridge, though if the weather should prove very warm and good, I hope it will encourage and strengthen you too.

I suppose I shall have one young turkey to nurse about that time, for I set a turkey hen last Wednesday upon 14 eggs because I wouldn't have an bad one which made me let you know it, that you may wish me good luck, Miss Cremer gave me my turkeys and would have me try, because she has managed hers so well that she had three fine broods of one turkey last year, but if I have three turkeys 'twill be very well.

The lady you mentioned is so gay she can't fail of charming now, but I think the charms of Miss Betty didn't stay long with the Justice. I was amazed to hear of the other. As for Jack and his lady, they are quite stupid I think, for we have heard nothing from them since we saw 'em.

Mrs Newton and one of her daughters were here at the mart, she's a jolly old lady and her daughter a pretty sort of woman, a young widow, they invited me much to Cambridge. She has sent me a piece of saffron half as broad as the table because I happened to say I wanted some. Tell my cousin Johnson I didn't send the petticoat, for I thought it would be lost, for the coachman was going to London as soon as he got to Norwich, but I design to send it by the first person that comes from Denton that will be troubled with it, it was too big for Mr Brock I thought, and I suppose it will never come amiss, and she shall have it.

I was at Sandringham last Saturday and Mrs Hoste gave me an account of the assemblies at Lynn Mart. She and Miss Hoste were there a week, but once going to the assembly was enough, for there the ladies were sat, of each side of a long table, very demurely, till the gentlemen had stared at 'em a good while, and were so kind to take them for partners. Mrs Hoste said it put her in mind of a petty sessions and looked as if they came to be hired. Then they danced most wretchedly and upon an old ragged green cloth to cover a bad floor, so they romped over the holes. Miss Hoste told me a comical story of Sir Edmund Bacon[32] of Gillingham, which I suppose you have heard, of his meeting the widow Suckling's[33] coach with her man thrown off the box, and the foreglass broke, and she thrown upon the braces, and he rode past and only said, 'What a devil madam could make it come into your head to drive your own coach?'

I have got a new packet and petticoat and I am going to make one of the Bath mobs,[34] for I think they are very pretty either down or up, and Mrs Newton gave me a martage of a new rowel.[35] I do think they look very well now, but I hated them at first when they stood up so much. How do you like the setting up the hoops,[36] they make the clothes hang well if they be done decently. One must set up their heads and tails to now look like the rest of the world. I think I am grown very fashionable to like all this, but I have been wondered at for not getting a little hood of velvet or some sort, but I think it's more a wonder anybody should like such nasty frightful things. Mrs Steglemen or somebody has put Mrs Golby on one. Tell my mother she look like a little headed man in it.

I wish you were here now to eat some little sucking rabbits not much bigger than mice and as fat as butter. When my brother come I'll send you half a dozen, or a dozen if I can get them just then, they'll soon be plentiful here. We have a sort of a neighbour coming into Mr Sharpe's[37] house, young Mr Davy. I suppose my father know who he is. I hope I shall get you a gown soon .

32. Sir Edmund Bacon 5th Baronet (1693-1738) of Gillingham. M.P. for Thetford 1727-1734, Oct. 1738: Sedgwick, I, p. 426.

33. Robert Suckling of Woodton (1673-1734) was 'said to have married Dorothy, daughter of John Berney of Swardston': Walter Rye, *Norfolk Families* (Norwich 1913), p. 869.

34. Women's indoor caps worn throughout the eighteenth century 'varying in shape and size with changing hair styles': A Buck, op. cit. p. 226.

35. A spiked revolving disk at the end of a spur, in this instance bought as a present at a market.

36. Circles of elastic material for expanding a woman's skirts.

37. John Sharpe (1706-1797?), Rector of West Newton 1732-1797, Sandringham and Babingley 1732-1797: Venn, IV, p. 49.

Woman Standing and Man Standing
*Engraved by Louis Philippe Boitard from paintings by Bartholomew Dandridge
in François Nivelon's 'Rudiments of Genteel Behaviour', 1737.
By courtesy of the Witt Library, Courtauld Institute, London.*

From Elizabeth Postlethwaite
Denton, c.1736

Dear Sister,

It is a great satisfaction to me to hear you are so well. I can't say this hot weather agree so well with me, it make me faint. That week Mr Brock was at Dersingham I was pretty much out of order with my cough, I was forced to lay a blister[38] on, I thank God I am better now.

I am sorry my brother should expose himself in that poor mean way, especially at Mr Houghton's. I am afraid my father will never be persuaded to give him any money for his pocket, there is money wanted for so many things there is no occasion for. We had company the other day at dinner and then there was several things wanting, china plates and more silver spoons. So there will be none to spare for him.

Miss Barry is something better, she think she is stronger but her voice is just the same. Last week here was the widow Lady Bacon and her two daughters and Mrs Betty Castle, they came with Mrs Sayer. Give my service to Miss and tell her I think she is quite wrong in choice of her music for your bees - the fire pan and tongs will be much more agreeable to them than the organ,[39] and what you are a spinning she may play, so there will be no time lost.

Tabby left her hood here, I gave it? Her father is got very well again. I think the little wish very pretty. I thank you for the holland, it will do mighty well.

From Elizabeth Postlethwaite
Denton, 14 October 1737

Dear Sister,

I received your kind letter last week, for which I give you thanks and for the bed gown you sent me. I wonder you should mention the

38. The practice of blistering was used not only against coughs, but for swellings, inflammation of the eyes and stomach, and even for toothache and fevers: Buchan, pp.192, 201, 262, 269, 288, 291, 359.

39. See *Kilvert's Diary 1870-1879, Selections form the Diary of the Rev. Francis Kilvert* (1944) William Plomer (ed.), p. 38 where Kilvert's father says that 'the Churchwarden John Bryant came after a swarm of his [bees] to the Church Ascension Day, clinking a frying pan and shovel.' It was widely believed that this noise would have a calming effect on the bees, persuading them to settle.

being pieced, I think it very handsome and a great deal too good for me. I shall always grudge to wear it. I put it on that night it came, it fit me very well. My mother was in the chamber when it was opened, she look out of temper at it but said nothing.

I have almost done the screen but couldn't have finished it without those feathers you sent, they make the greatest show of any of them. There is nothing drawn in the middle part, I wanted the Dr.[40] I put only peacocks feathers and pheasants there so that I think it look a little like a sunflower. I wanted your fancy in it. One of our coach horses are lame, so I hope that and the bad roads will prevent Mrs Townshend coming to Denton this Winter, we are much better without her.

My father have had a letter from the Dr since he have been at Cambridge. He said the weather was so uncertain he couldn't tell when he should be at Dersingham. It must be very uncomfortable for you to be so much alone, I should have rejoiced to have seen you come in a boat, I would soon have been ready to have gone back with you. I thank God for it I have held pretty well and free from coughing a good while now. All this dismal wet weather had no bad effect upon me at all. I am sorry for Mrs Cremer, you have so few good neighbours, she must be a great loss to you.

We all join in due respects to yourself and Dr, I hope he is come home by this time. If be not, tell him when you write to him, heartily wish him a good journey. Pray tell your maid I thank her for the feathers.

From Elizabeth Postlethwaite
Denton, 20 August 1738

Dear Sister,

I would have wrote before now, but the hot weather prevented me, it disagreed with me very much. I was fit for nothing but to lie upon the bed all day long. I am afraid it must make you very faint, everybody here was just dead with heat.

We have got Mrs Townshend again as I thought we should. I believe she design taking this for her home but hope it will be too dull for her always to live here, I suppose our neighbours are not polite nor

40. i.e. Elizabeth wished the Dr would draw something for her on the screen.

great enough to make visiting agreeable to her. She talk as if she designed to visit Lady Turner.[41] My mother and she are to meet her at the Ditchingham assembly. Dr Gooch and lady[42] and little master and three servants are to come next week to stay about a fortnight or three weeks. My poor aunt Goodwin had the misfortune about a month ago to break her other arm. She was not sensible what she suffered with it, she complained very little. She have a miserable life, it would be happy for her if it pleased God to take her out of the world.

I got this receipt which I have sent you of Mrs Townshend, she recommended it to Mrs Houghton as very good to strengthening the blood. I thought it might be of service to you if you like to try it. She say she would have write to you and sent it herself, but that you owe her a letter. You must write a letter full of compliments to get into favour again if you think it worth doing, for she is very angry at present though your inviting of her to Dersingham have done some good. I think of you daily and want as often to see you.

The Receipt

Take three handfuls of red sage, stamp it in a stone mortar very small, put it into a quart of red port and let stand 3 or 4 days close covered, then strain it out and bottle it. Take three spoonfuls of it and four spoonfuls of running water in a morning, fasting till the claret be done.[43] This is good for scurvy and spleen.

Hannah and Biddy both go away. Hannah gave my Mother warning which she was very angry at a little while, but you know the servants are not long out of favour. I don't think you can read what I have write to you though I take the liberty of paying my respects though I have not had the pleasure of hearing from you a long time. This I have several times had thoughts of doing when I considered what an insignificant letter my last to you was, though I hope I then made the true excuse for it that I had a great deal of company and I believe that was all the letter, for I remember it was so very much like nothing that I was afraid I couldn't expect favour of one from you, as for an answer it was impossible to that.

41. Mary, daughter of Sir William Blois of Grundisburgh, Suffolk, second wife of Sir Charles Turner. His first wife, Mary, sister of Sir Robert Walpole, had died in April 1701, having borne him four daughters: Sedgwick, II, p. 486.

42. Hannah, daughter of Sir John Miller 4th Baronet, of Lavant, Sussex, Thomas Gooch's second wife: D.N.B VIII, pp. 109-110.

43. Port, surely?

From Barbara Kerrich
Dersingham, 31 January 1739

Dear Sister,

I soon recovered that disorder though I was very ill for three days. I think I am like Will Whitson, now very ill, or very well, for everybody tell me I grow fat and look healthful. I believe my cold did me good, I had so great a discharge from my head for above a fortnight and it couldn't reach my stomach for I had no passage from my head that way all the time.

You have made me in two minds about my mantle, Miss Hoste's is black lined with ermine which look mighty well only it's made short before, and that sort I don't like. Mrs Hoste's is cut in a mighty pretty manner and come as low as the knee, I believe I shall have black made so.

I happened of a small set of china such as you were wishing for, and I hope they will come safe to you. I design to be very careful in putting them up. You must not invite anybody that love a great deal of tea at a time, though they hold more than they seem to do and are not exactly sized.[44]

I have a great many letters to write and the chief topic of all must be about myself as my father and all were so kind to inquire after my health, so excuse the shortness yourself and make the same reason do for the rest. My brother sent no letter to answer. I am very glad he is got well again and hope we shall hear from him one time or other, or see him here, he's a great stranger.

I have sent you *The History of Joseph*..... The china is seasoned.

From Elizabeth Postlethwaite
Denton, 18 March 1739

Dear Sister,

I thank you for your kind letter and I should have wrote sooner had I been able. I thank God I have now pretty well recovered that fit of coughing and have had no returns since I was bled and blistered then, so hope I shall be free from it for sometime. You are very

---

44. 'They are mighty neat and pretty, I drink tea out of no other. You put them up so well, they came all very safe': Ms 589, f.16 Elizabeth Postlethwaite to Barbara Kerrich, 16 March 1739.

The Gough Family

(1741)
Oil painting by
William Verelst
(private loan)
Victoria & Albert
Museum, London
By courtesy of the
V & A Picture Library

The Game of Quadrille (c. 1743)
Engraved by Louis Truchy from a painting by Francis Hayman
By courtesy of the Witt Library, Courtauld Institute, London

sensible it is always a great pleasure to me to hear from you, if you had nothing to tell me but that you were well would be enough: I should think your letters worth paying for.

I suppose you are a topping gamester by this time. Mrs Townshend sent you a full and perfect receipt for ombre,[45] we play every day that I'm quite weary of it - I hate to see the cards. But then after tea she read Sir Philip Sidney[46] which makes amends, for I think it is worth anybody's reading.

My mother found out your Christmas trick, it is very pretty. We have got Hannah again, for she that came at Michaelmas is gone away with child by the fellow. They were married last week. I don't know whether he is to go away, he is another Ammi. Goody Shimon desire you to tell Sarah her brother Robin have broke his leg; I believe he is like to do very well. I am weary, or I would send you some poetry of Miss Peak's[47] upon friendship. My father design writing next week to the Dr.

From Elizabeth Postlethwaite
Denton, July 1739

Dear Sister,

It is a very great disappointment to me your not coming at all this Summer. I was in hopes you might have come with safety in the chariot, but since it can't be must content myself and hope you will let me hear the oftener from you.

I have sent some remnants of edgings as you desired, all Mrs Kerrich had that was fit for the purpose and those few things I have made which I desire you to accept. I wish you may like them. My mother didn't like the cutting of the little shirts you sent so I bought a piece of holland for a couple, but I had not time to make the other. I have been a very sorry help to you, I assure my will was good, if my strength had, to have done a great deal more. I have sent you a blanket that is made of piece of one of my own petticoats. I have sent back 4 yards of the gingham my father ordered Mr Brock to pay for my gown.

---

45. Mrs Townshend had obligingly sent Barbara details of the rules. The game required three players using 40 cards, the 'ombre' being the player who undertook to win the pool: Ms 589, f. 241, 1732; Harvey, p. 595.

46. Sir Philip Sidney (1554-86), poet and soldier. Harvey, p. 754.

47. Miss Peak was probably an unpublished writer whose verses had a local circulation only and may be the lady who married Mr Gains: see below, p.111.

Miss Barry lost my little duck within two days after she had it. She fancy a kite got it. We are to keep two servants more at Michaelmas. There is a maid hired for me the time I keep my chamber and a man, for my father intend gathering all his tithes his self. He is going to buy cart and horses and all things that are wanting, but you know he is so unfit for business I fancy he will soon be weary of it.[48] I am afraid the Dr forgot to finish your picture .

From Elizabeth Postlethwaite
Denton, 14 December 1739

Dear Sister,

I hope you will excuse my not writing sooner, which I designed a long time ago, but my father's and mother's writing hinder me.

I like my locks mightily so well that I never go without them, the colour suit exactly. I am quite sick of the honey water, I believe it would have made me as grey as a cat if I had gone on with it. When the Bishop was here he was very civil, he came up to speak to me and brought Mr Gooch[49] up with him. We had two coachfuls, Mr Fowle[50] and his lady and the youngest Miss Turner, and Mr Playter that married her sister. I had all the ladies above with me. Miss Yeats carried it with a great deal of freedom and good nature. She came running up as soon as she had dined and sat with me till tea time. Mrs Gooch ask after you, she had on the prettiest silk I ever see.

Mrs Louson is dead and her husband make a very grand burying for her, and had her lay in state 4 days. She had two mutes and wax candles burning all the time. I was as great a stranger to Miss Fairman's present as you, I suppose it will not be the last. I sent Mrs Houghton's letter to Mr Kerrich.

48. Within a few years Mrs Postlethwaite was managing the accounts, 'which your father, poor man, never did': Ms 586, f. 182 Matilda Postlethwaite to Barbara Kerrich, 20 Aug. 1742.

49. Sir Thomas Gooch 3rd Baronet (1720-1781), son of Thomas Gooch, Bishop of Norwich, 2nd Baronet, and his first wife, Mary, daughter of William Sherlock, Dean of St Paul's. Two portraits of Sir Thomas Gooch by John Theodore Heins and Thomas Hudson (lots 144 and 145 respectively) were sold at the Benacre Hall Sale: G.E.C., V, p. 92; Introduction, n.17 above.

50. Thomas Fowle LL.D (1696-1755), Commissary to the Dean and Chapter of Norwich and to the Archdeacon of Norfolk 1731: Venn, II, p. 167.

From Elizabeth Postlethwaite
Denton, 1 March 1740

Dear Sister,

Since you are grown so great a quadrille[51] player I thought you would want fish and counters. I have sent 4 dozen fish and 3 dozen counters, they are not very neat but I could get no better, and I have sent a basket. Mrs Dalling had one of those Pope Joan tables,[52] but they never play. I asked Miss Nanny for it, she told me she would bring it.

The very severe weather we have had made me cough a great deal. I was blooded and had two blisters, I thank God I am got pretty well again now. I was pleased to hear you are grown so hardy as to be able to bear it to walk in, for I think there never was such weather ever felt. I was ready to freeze by the fire.

I hope you have got me a pair of shoes for I have none to wear. I desire you would wear them the time Mr Brock is there. I am glad you like Betty Brady so well, you may tell her and Tabby their sister Mary have got a girl. She live with her brother Tom. I shall hope to hear by Mr Brock the time of your coming. Pray bring little Martin[53] with you if you can any way contrive it, I must see him.

From Elizabeth Postlethwaite
Denton, Spring 1740 ?

Dear Sister,

I shall be glad to hear by Mr Brock you are got rid of your disorder, but I hope it's only the effects of your cold and then it will do you good, which is a general complaint. I have had one that put me a good deal out of order, and a tickling cough. I was forced to lay on a blister but it did not bring my old cough. I thank God I am pretty well again now.

51. A game played by four people, with 40 cards It replaced ombre as the fashionable game c.1726, and was in turn superseded by whist. The counters and fishes were used for stakes: Harvey, p. 675.

52. 'A pleasant and amusing game and well worth learning,...but has the disadvantage of requiring a special board to play it': H. E. Heather, *Cards and Card Tricks* (n.d.), pp. 169-173.

53. 'Little Martin' a son of Sarah, Barbara Kerrich's nurse.

Miss Sukey is with us yet, and is like to be, for the smallpox is still very much at Bungay.[54] My mother is very civil to her and have given her a lining for a black velvet mantle which she have got made up. We play at ombre every night, but we want Mrs Townshend's letter. My mother desire you to send it. A blue velvet mantle trimmed with gold frogs, to be sure, will look very handsomely, but I should like a black one trimmed in the same manner better. My garden look very pretty, one flower have been out this fortnight, them that are in mould are not out yet. I have made up that fine edging you sent me, it make a very handsome mob. I don't think the other so bad as you talk on.

Miss Nanny Dalling have got a spark, I can assure, and would do very well if she were few years older. It is young Mr Lindsey, he is rich and sober. I believe Mr Dalling don't know anything of it yet. I suppose when he do he will nip his self to dead, he will be so pleased. My mother told you of Miss Langley's match. Mr Paston talk of binding him to a baker, but he is such a sorry poor creature he is hardly fit for anything, he have a withered arm and leg and no brains.[55] I shall hope to see you and the Dr in May. I have sent three of the books, you can never read this letter.

From Barbara Kerrich
Dersingham, 5 July 1740

Dear Sister,

I wrote to my mother last Monday by the post and told her how finely well I am at present, though I have had pain of my teeth two nights since, but hope it is gone off again. I had nothing of it last night, I am very much obliged to Mrs Smith for inquiring so much after me, but don't know how to apply the oil of paper, I think I know how to make it, burning it between two plates. I am not certain how forward I am with child, I think I quickened very early, which I am told is a good sign of having it born alive. I pray God it may. I couldn't be above 15 or 16 weeks gone then and it is 5 weeks ago next

54. Perhaps it was during this visit that she gave her friend Elizabeth 'a bird which she had at Bungay, it's a King Harry and sing prettily. It sound 'Miss Postlethwaite' as plain as possible for any creature that don't directly speak'. Sukey had stayed at the rectory a month during a previous smallpox outbreak: Ms 588, f. 149 Matilda Postlethwaite to Barbara Kerrich, Spring 1740; f. 141, 11 Dec. 1738.

55. The unfortunate Mr Jennings died of smallpox in 1742: Ms 589, f. 38, 16 July 1742.

Sunday since I was sensible of the time, because I was very near fainting.

The Dr is gone to Lynn, he went yesterday that he might have an opportunity of waiting of the Bishop last night because today his Lordship will be so much engaged, old Mr Pyle[56] told us he was to lie at his house. Miss Cremer is here, she came to stay with me last night because I was alone. She is my best neighbour still. Mrs Gregson is a perfect maggot[57] and a very odd temper. I have lately had a visit from Dr Browne's lady and daughter and Recorder Berney and his lady are coming to see me very soon. I saw her t'other day, I think she is a very agreeable woman. She asked me if the lady her brother was to have were handsome, for she had heard one of the Dean's daughters was a very great beauty.

Mrs Hoste was taken very ill last Monday and Dr Browne was sent for. He called to see me as he came from thence and he told me he fancied it would prove to be a breeding fit. If it should, I don't know but Sarah may be the wet nurse, for Mrs Hoste think Sarah's are the finest thrifty children that ever were seen. The Major said she might nurse for a prince. I am to write a letter to Sarah's mother which she desire you would send to her 'tis to desire one of her sisters to come to her at Michaelmas.

I hope my father will be so kind to come and see me when Mr Brock come again. I give you a great many thanks for your kind presents and think the fan is wonderful pretty and you have made me a very neat housewife. I wish you had made one of it for yourself. The handkerchief I like better than any I ever saw of the sort. You did not tell me what it cost. Calimanco[58] is just ready to foal. Since I wrote to my mother, the Dr thinks 'that dish that never was above ground before' is fish.

From Barbara Kerrich
Dersingham, 30 November 1740

Dear Sister,

I wrote to my mother last week but my letters are not worthy having now, for I can talk of nothing nor think of nothing but the loss

---

56. Thomas Pyle (1675-1756), Minister of St. Nicholas Lynn 1701; Lecturer and Curate of St Margaret's Lynn 1711-1732; Vicar 1732-1755: Venn, III, p. 410.

57. Whimsical.

58. Barbara Kerrich's mare.

of my poor child which I had fixed my affections upon too soon.[59] You'll wonder to hear me say it, but I believe if I hadn't the best of husbands it would almost break my heart. But he never leave me, and is always contriving to divert me from thoughts of it. I once thought I couldn't have been concerned for a child, especially an infant, and I dare say I shall be reckoned silly enough for it by those that have children, but where there is none the case is very different. I can't bear to see Sarah's young child yet. Though I am always thus uneasy, I am grown as strong and well as ever I was in my life. I shall be glad to hear that you hold well .

From Elizabeth Postlethwaite
Denton, 7 May 1741

Dear Sister,

I am very glad to find by my mother's letter you intend taking your drink which I hope will have a good effect, don't be discouraged but make yourself easy and leave the event to Providence, but pray have another midwife. Though seeing you and the Dr is the only pleasure I have, yet I don't nor can't desire it, because I am sure it would be a great deal too much for you.

My father and mother were at Mr Barry's last week, there they met Mr and Mrs Stillingfleet,[60] I don't hear she is breeding yet. Justice Kerrich's lady was brought to bed last Tuesday of a daughter and Mrs Farrow[61] on Saturday of a daughter. I thank God I hold pretty well. My mother intend writing next week. Goodman Brady want to know how his daughters do.

59. Her stepmother expressed great concern, adding: 'though you know we're not over fond of children, but I do assure I was very desirous you should have enjoyed this, had it pleased God, but He knows what's best for us': Ms 588, f. 157, 14 Nov. 1740.

60. Fairfax Stillingfleet (1703-1755), Rector of Alburgh 1729-1755. A 'jolly, hearty man' who in his youth courted Barbara Kerrich. Mrs Postlethwaite was deeply mistrustful of him: Venn, IV, p. 163; Ms 588, f. 129 Matilda Postlethwaite to Barbara Kerrich, Spring 1736; f. 238, 27 April 1752.

61. Anne Dalling married John Farrow of St George, Colgate, Norwich at Denton 16 June 1741: NRO PD 136/4.

From Barbara Kerrich
Dersingham, 24 May 1741

Dear Sister,

I wrote to my mother last week to give an account that we had a very good journey home, the water was so low at that bridge that is taken up we could easily go over it, the coachman knowing the water. The Dr would have wrote to my father this week but he is to set out early tomorrow morning for Cambridge, but intends to be at home about the middle of next week again.

I wish your way was here, I intend to spend a whole day with Miss Cremer and another with Mrs Bogges and walk about and divert myself. Mrs Gregson and I are to go to Snettisham-Stone by the seaside that I was telling you on, that I hope with all this I shan't think of the time so long.

We had a person taken ill in the town t'other day which had like to have stopped his journey. A girl that had been out of order almost a week and was thought to be breeding the rash, but it proves the smallpox. He's a very good sort, they live upon the Common, a good distance from us that I am not at all afraid, but the Dr was vastly uneasy about it at first. He have ordered everything before he go and one that has had it, to carry things that they want to their door and sent for Mr Exton to direct her mother how to manage her. She has had it, but they are very poor and very silly. There is but one more in that family to have it. Some poor families there are near them, but I hope with care it will be stopped.

I went to Sandringham last Friday in that gown you gave me. Mrs Hoste admired it very much, she said it was a mighty pretty silk. I got a pattern for your hat, I design to go to work on it tomorrow. Mrs Branthwayt and Miss[62] were at Mrs Gregson's last week and Miss Branthwayt was telling me of a new way of cutting these hats, something of a slope from the hind part that ties under the chin, which I fancy could be very pretty for you, but she hadn't it with her. So I must cut it by Mrs Hoste's pattern as well as I can. Miss Branthwayt was here in a very handsome night gown, but such a modey[63] sleeve as I never saw. It was as long as any old woman's that ever you see in your life, quite hid the bent of her arm, and the upper part of the cuff loose from the sleeve, quite round.

62. Possibly the wife and daughter of John Branthwayte (1697-1766), Rector of Kettlestone 1721-1766: Venn, I p. 207.

63. 'A la mode' -fashionable, rather than alamode – 'a thin silk of plain weave originally lustred and usually black': A. Buck, op. cit., p. 225.

Molly was a very good hussy for me in my absence. I have said nothing to her yet, only today I told her that when Sarah was gone to Sandringham she must think of doing more in the kitchen when I have company, or else it would never do. She said Betty would do what she had a mind for, all her (?) and therefore her helping would signify nothing. I shall tell you more when Mr Brock come.

I shall write till I have no room to do it up, but I must tell you how often Johnny ask for you, he can't make it out how he come to be so far from you, I dare say, not a day have passed since we came from you, but he has asked twenty times, 'Where's Miss Detts, where's Miss Detts? I can't find her', especially in a morning, then he say 'What's Miss Detts doing?' I fancy he think of his breakfasting with you, and sometimes he says he'll go into the coach and find you again. He never ask for anybody else, only one day he told his mother Madam Postlethwaite would be angry with her if she fight him.

I have ten young turkeys. My bees swarmed yesterday, the first that have hereabouts. I went to two or three shops to get you some French plums but could hear of none and I desired Mrs Rice to go and look at some other places after I was gone.

From Barbara Kerrich
Dersingham, St John Baptist 24 June 1741

Dear Sister,

I have sent you the little kettle and lamp, as you said you should like either of them. 'Tis very light and pretty to handle, but was full small for me but hold more than one would think it does by the look. I like your gown prodigiously, it's the prettiest thing of the sort that ever I saw, and I fancy strong, for it seems a mighty good cloth.

Last Saturday sennight, Sarah was brought to bed of another boy, a very pretty small child the very picture of Johnny. She had the best time that ever she had and is got well already. Tabby was her nurse, for as she sell flour she was afraid to trust anybody in her house. She didn't know right well, but however in 3 or 4 days she was weighing of flour herself. Tabby miscarried a little while ago. I believe it's the first time she have been with child. She was about twelve weeks gone, but she says she was so ill she can never go through with so much again.

Johnny is now come to me, and of his own accord, bid me tell you he will be very good and would have you come and see him now. Sarah's other child, Tommy, is a poor weak thing still. My maid Molly have undertaken to dip him in cold water every morning.[64] She has done it three mornings, the poor child begin to be sadly afraid. Last Tuesday I had something of the colic, but else I hold very well. I expect to lie in sometime in October, I always have laid in about that time of the year.

Now I must tell you what a fine show of ladies and gentlemen we had at church last Sunday. Mrs Hoste and Mrs Nelthorpe, the Major and Mr Nelthorpe,[65] and Mr William Hoste[66] who preached there were all our guests; and in Mr Gregson's seat was Dr Browne's lady and daughter, who are always as fine as jewels and rich clothes can make them. They are come to stay a week with Mrs Gregson, but they didn't come in with us on Sunday, for Mrs Hoste I think, has left off visiting Mrs Gregson. Mr Nelthorpe had on the beautifullest waistcoat I ever saw - wrought upon white Padusoy,[67] full of exceeding small flowers of the finest colours and embroidered round very thick with gold broader than an orrice[68] in a wave fashion. Johnny was highly delighted with it and Mr Nelthorpe was as much pleased with him. He said he was the finest child he ever saw in his life and had the most command of words for his age. He does apply words surprisingly well indeed, and describe anything very cleverly, and looked so unconcerned and talked away so prettily, he made them all laugh. Mrs Browne and Miss Browne come almost everyday to see me and sometimes twice a day and to hear Molly sing, who has a very sweet voice, and sings very well. She begin to be brisk again now.

I believe Ruth Brady is to be dairymaid to Mrs Davy at Michaelmas.[69] Betty and Mary stay where they are. Sarah's sister Nan is very much liked for dairymaid at Sandringham, and I believe stay. Mrs Gregson never paid her wages yet. Pray when you have an opportunity, find that piece of my gown.

---

64 It was accepted medical practice to treat sickly children in this way. Edward Montagu underwent a similar dowsing when just over a year old, in 1714: Isabel Grundy (ed.), *Lady Mary Wortley Montagu: Selected Letters* (Harmondsworth Middlesex 1997) , p. 117 n.5.

65. James Nelthorpe, natural son of James Nelthorpe of Lynford Hall: Sedgwick , II, p. 291.

66. William Hoste (b. 1718), son of James Hoste of Sandringham: Foster, II, p. 696.

67. A strong corded silk fabric, much worn in the eighteenth century.

68. Kinds of gold or silver lace or embroidery.

69. The Feast of St Michael, 29th September, a date on which servants used to be hired: Harvey, p. 540.

From Elizabeth Postlethwaite
Denton, 7 August 1741

Dear Sister,

I had wrote by Shimon, but I didn't know time enough of his going to Dersingham. My mother's letter was wrote to send by the post. I was surprised and vexed to find by your letter to my mother that she should huff you for sending the wash ball, indeed, she was angry, but I couldn't have thought she would have wrote about it. I wash my hands with it every day now.

She is gone to Norwich, she stay about three weeks, the Bishop's chariot came for her last Monday. My cousin Johnson is with me. I think Miss Hoste's thought was very comical and pretty. I have pretty well recovered my going downstairs and often use my hat to stand at the windows in. Mrs Blyford have got an ivory hat but hers is not made like the Leghorn ones, it look more like shells – it's spotted with blue. Dr Kerrich's[70] lady is at Harleston and one of her sisters, they were to go to Norwich this week to make a visit at the palace. My cousin Johnson bid me tell you the Dr should have had his wig before now, but her son have not been able to do any work since you see him. I am mighty well pleased with the plays you sent me. My cousin Postlethwaite[71] is now here, he tell me that he and Miss Jenny and Mr Jack Kerrich[72] and his wife intend being at Dersingham the week after the next. I find little Johnny have not forgot me yet, I often wish him here. Tell him when Mr Brock come I will send him money to buy him another pair of shoes, but he mustn't cut them a pieces.

From Elizabeth Postlethwaite
Denton, 27 August 1741

Dear Sister,

I return you thanks for your kind present of fruit. They were very good, the peaches were a little bruised though they were so well done up. A scarcity of fruit is everybody's complaint. Mrs Dalling have none.

---

70. Dr John Kerrich M.D.

71. Mathew Postlethwaite (1716-1760) son of John Postlethwaite of Millum, Cumberland: Foster, III, p. 1134.

72. John Kerrich (1708-1774?), a younger half brother of Samuel Kerrich; Rector of Banham 1735-1772; Vicar of Buchanton St. Martin 1745-1774: Venn, III, p. 10.

I am glad you are determined to keep a chariot, if it were only that we should see the Dr and you with less trouble and charge. You may tell Mr Cremer I don't know anybody to speak to for a wife for him but if he be resolved to have a wife hereabouts, he must come his self and see for one. I have not seen Miss Sukey, if he will have her, he must keep her chaise and a boy to wait on her. My father and mother come home tonight. Mr Lakers is dead, he was buried on Wednesday. I thank you for the receipts, they are both very good, the pudding is as good as ever I ate. Mrs Wright of Alburgh is now come to make me a visit.

From Elizabeth Postlethwaite
Denton, 13 September 1741

Dear Sister,

I think Mrs Houghton have made you a very friendly visit at last. She wrote her sister word she was mightily pleased with being at Dersingham, but I don't see how she could have proposed seeing much about it if it hadn't happened that Mrs Browne was with you. I think it is a very odd fancy in her, she won't keep no coach horses, she may as well give you her chariot, it can do her no manner of good except she keep it to look on or touch.

My mother is out almost every day, she is returning all her visits before Winter. She was last Monday at Mrs Arrowsmith's. She say she will not entertain no more sparks, they come by the half year together and make nothing on it, so I think Mr Cremer had better take a wife where he is, Miss Sukey only laugh at him. Will Sarah make as fine a child for Mrs Hoste as her own little boy Johnny? I have sent him half-a-crown for a pair of shoes, but tell him if he cut them a pieces must go without. Hannah have sent him some comfits.[73]

I have sent you a *Pamela* fan, I wish they had made her look better where she is getting out at the window, she cut a sad figure.[74] They have drawn Mother Jewkes well, she look like what she is, she have a fine broad face. The account you give of the storm is very terrible, we had a little of the same storm here about 2 o'clock in the afternoon. I

73. Sweetmeats, sugar plums.
74. *Pamela, or Virtue Rewarded*, a novel by Samuel Richardson, published in 1740. Such was its popularity that fans were sold illustrating characters from the book. Elizabeth Postlethwaite was given the 3rd edition by her father: Harvey, p. 611; Ms 589, f. 37, 27 March 1742.

Pamela in the custody of Mrs Jewkes (1745)
Engraved by Antoine Benoist from a painting by Joseph Highmore
By courtesy of the Witt Library, Courtauld Institute, London

Printed below the picture in English and in French:

*'Pamela, being now in the custody of Mrs Jewkes, seizes an occasion
(as they are walking in the garden) to propose a correspondence with Mr
Williams, in order to contrive an Escape, who agree to hide their
letters between two tiles near the Sunflower.'*

am sorry you are not well, let me hear by Mr Brock how you do. Take no notice when you write I sent Johnny anything.

From Barbara Kerrich
Dersingham, 24 September - 8 October 1741

Dear Sister,

Now I begin to expect Mr Brock and shall be glad to hear how you do, I have got the things ready for him. There's two yards of the fine edging, so I hope it will do very well.

My cousin Johnson was very brisk when we were at Norwich, talking of their late election they have had for Sheriff,[75] and teasing me to send the gown and shift. I told her I would not, but she said she would come to the coachman and see what he had got for her when he came back. However, there was nothing worth her going for. I sent only a shift and apron because she would go for something. Her daughter said she was sure my goodness was such that I would send them. She talk like a player and look a masquerade, for she have shaved her forehead at top. I suppose she had a large widow's peak, you never saw anything look so blue and frightful in your life, except you had seen Tom Andrews with a fringed mob on. She was very well dressed else, with a clean blue and white cross-barred gown and clean apron. She dined with us, and the Dr gave her half-a-crown, she took eleven shillings for my coat.

When I came home I found everything in very good order, and Tabby in particular was glad to see me. In the letter I wrote to my mother I sent word she was to stay, to prevent her brother's coming with Mr Brock. Little Martin had forgot me at first, but now he is never easy but when he is here. Sarah say he plague her out of her life, he don't like her victuals, for she would have gave him some pork pie that had apples in it. He said it would make him sick, he must go see his mistress, then he should have mutton and capers and all. We had a wild young lady here last week that almost frightened him out of his wits, that I believe if he could have reached high enough he would have knocked on the head with Mr Punch. He gave her a good rap when she sat down by him. What affronted him most, was her running after him and covering him with her hoop petticoat. She came hither

75. The sheriffs were chosen the last Tuesday in August and sworn in on Michaelmas day: John Calver and William Crowe were elected sheriffs for 1741. Blomefield, III, p. 450 n.2.

with Mr Goodrich: he brought here two ladies and a gentleman to look of Whistler's house in order to buy it. They hadn't heard of the smallpox having been there and one of ladies was prodigiously afraid, and Mr Goodrich said we must be good Samaritans to them and give 'em lodgings in their necessity. The gentleman's name is Lucas, he lives sometimes at Brackendale, but I believe my father don't know him.

I had wrote thus far a fortnight ago and expected Mr Brock both the Mondays till it was too late to finish it and send it to Lynn for last Monday. Skerry said he fully expected him, but I'll send it tomorrow if he does not come before Gooden Miller calls for the letters, for I am sure you must think me very negligent and abominably so in not writing to you all this while.

Now I must tell you about my garden: the greens are almost all cut down, only what stand properly, and are very fine ones. The two Goliaths and their wives were demolished first and then a yew hedge that stood right against the parlour windows and hindered our seeing into the knot, which indeed look now very pretty. The Dr have bestowed a deal of cost and pains on it, for Martin and our new man worked hard above a fortnight about it. I hope we have got a very clever man servant, he seems so at present, he lay a cloth and wait at table mighty well, and is not the least conceited of his own ways which is a great wonder, for he is a very smart looking fellow. I never saw anything of his laying a cloth, but that night Mr Goodrich's company was here, but I thought he went about it very handily. He tell Molly he can set up napkins in the shape of the whole criss-cross row. Molly and Tabby agree better than they did and when they don't I take no notice on it.

My calf is grown a fine one and eat bran and oats very prettily. The milk we give it still is almost as good as the milk from the cow, for we let but one meal stand at a time that that is milked at night. We fleet[76] in the morning, so it never stand but 12 hours, if it stood 24 as it used to do, the milk wouldn't be good enough for it yet. We get but a little butter at present, Tabby have churned about two pound at a time. I have a little churn coming home such as they have that churn every morning for breakfast. You desired me to tell you all I could about my calf and everything, 'tis a sad nonsensical letter, don't let it be seen.

Mrs Hoste came again last Friday and made me a very kind visit, brought Mr and Mrs Hammond with her on purpose, that they might

76. 'To fleet milk, to skim it': Bailey

see what wanted to be done to the house, and they looked about and Mrs Hammond[77] said what I desired was very reasonable and it should be done in the Spring of the year. She brought 2 or 3 bags full of roots of flowers to set in the knot. They were all most prodigiously civil, and when she went away said she hoped she should see me at Wootton, which is a great deal from her. I'll send you some hyacinth roots by Mr Brock to set in your closet and you'll have them bloom at Christmas. You may set them either in water or mould in your glasses. I don't know but mould may do best in such glasses as yours, Mrs Hammond set them in water. She have Dutch glasses on purpose that are smallest in the middle so the root does not fall quite to the bottom, but the fibres have room to strike downward, you almost see how they grow. We have set some to stand upon the chimney piece, but your closet is warm enough, make your garden as soon as you have them.

I like my mob that I made like yours, better than anything I have to my head. Last Sunday was my wedding day and I put on all that suit of linen and my scarlet gown. I can tell you I made no small figure in our church. I pinned the mob up and put on my velvet hood that it looked like a Dutch head under that. I'll put a piece of my gown into the box that you may see how well 'tis dyed. I shall be glad to hear that my brother is safe, I find by my father's letter he has been in a great deal of danger. Now I think my letter begin to look like a lease, it's time to knock off, the Dr say he never saw such a heap of stuff in his life. If I be forced to send it by the post, and Curll[78] should get it and print it, 'twill make an ingenious pamphlet - there will be no occasion for a name for it.

From Elizabeth Postlethwaite
Denton, 15 October 1741

Dear Sister,

I received your letter with a great deal of pleasure to hear you are got so well, and that the Dr hold well this sickly time.

We had Justice Kerrich and his lady here last Monday, she is a very agreeable woman. Mrs Arrowsmith and Miss Sukey dined here that day. We had a good deal of talk about Mr Cremer. She don't seem to have any dislike to him, nor she won't own that ever she

77. Jane, daughter of Sir Walter Clarges, Ist Baronet: Sedgwick, II, p. 103.
78. Edmund Curll (1675-1747), bookseller and pamphleteer: Harvey, p. 209.

laughed at him. I believe if he will come and they can agree about her circumstances, she will like it very well. You may talk with him about it when you see him. Mrs Stillingfleet is got to housekeeping, Mrs Morse is to board with her. I have bought me linen for a gown, I think it is a pretty thing, it's only a single sprig,[79] it look like work. I fancy you would like it, if you want one I can get you one the same, I had it of Mrs Kerrich.

From Elizabeth Postlethwaite
Denton, October 1741

Dear Sister,

I designed writing sooner, but have not been well enough since my going downstairs till now, though I coughed but little it disordered my stomach very much, that it have quite discouraged me from trying any more this year. However, I was a great deal out of order last week with a swelled face, I laid on a blister that help to carry it off, I am pretty well again now.

Miss Sukey Arrowsmith's match is quite off, her gentleman have not used her handsomely, he wouldn't settle any part of his estate upon her. If she would have him without any security he would marry her, but not else. She say she think she is born not to be married. Miss Barry have been here. She is concerned she could see you the time you were at Denton. She is very brisk and merry, I hear she have hired two maids and a boy against she marry.

I am mightily pleased with my hat, it's so warm and I think the cut is handsomer than the small ones, and the colour don't signify for me, I shan't go abroad in it. I thank you for the wash ball, but I mustn't use it when my mother is at home. She can't bear the smell of it,[80] I like it very well.

Hannah stay, Anne and Betty go away, Mary Barnes came in Anne's place. I am very glad to hear the smallpox spread no further. I would not have you say anything in your letters but what may be seen. I am weary, I must have done. I would not have the Dr call your letter a heap of stuff. I should like as long a one every time you write. I thank him for the seals.

79. A design of twigs or small branches.

80. Mrs Postlethwaite equally disliked the smell of hyacinths, finding them 'too sweet': Ms 588, f. 149, Spring 1740.

From Barbara Kerrich
Dersingham, 23 November 1741(?)

Dear Sister,

I am mighty glad to hear you are grown better and I pray God continue it. Little Johnny is got quite well and I think I can almost see him grow since his illness, he says he'll nurse me as much as I did him if I be sick and be as little as he, or else he can't he says.

Mr and Miss Cremer dined here last Thursday and Mr Cremer toasted Miss Sukey's health and said he was going towards Norwich upon business, and had some thoughts of being at Bungay before he returned. But afterwards we happened to talk of good wives and marrying etc; and he said the best woman in the world, if he died for her, should never make him settle anything because all his own fortunes were in trade, and he could turn money to ten times more advantage that way than could be made on it any other. Which I believe he does, for he is reckoned to grow very rich, but I told him, if those were his real sentiments, he might as well think of going to the moon for a wife as to think of Miss Sukey. He said his affairs must take a very unhappy turn indeed if her thirds did not come to a great deal more than her fortune. I hope I have not quite discouraged him.[81]

I doubt I can't get my mother any morells[82] before next April, which is the time of gathering them. I have used a great many this year, and have but a very few left. I'll inquire of a man in this town that used to gather them and bring them to me. I have had none of him this year and if he has any now I will send them. Mrs Hoste gave me a great many last Spring, but I thought my mother had not liked them. I will take care and get all I can next Spring. One of the servants at Mr Hendry's died last night of the smallpox.

In all my letters I have wrote to you I forgot to tell you that Mrs

---

81. Clearly Mr Cremer felt that any marriage settlement made with Mrs Arrowsmith on behalf of Sukey, would cost him (and his eventual heirs), more than she could bring to the marriage in the form of a dowry. In the eighteenth century the traditional third of a husband's (or his family's) income that a widow could expect to receive on his death, was frequently modified by a marriage settlement which would merely give her a fixed income for life. Such jointures could be considerably less value than a dower, but became more common partly because of the difficulty in valuing estates as more people accumulated wealth in forms other than land. They also deprived the widow of any legal right over her late husband's estate: L. Stone, op. cit., pp. 72, 221; A. Laurence, op. cit., pp. 230-234.

82. 'An eatable fungus, much in request': Bailey.

Browne when she was here, would have me let her maid cut my hair behind. She learnt to cut hair at London and does it mighty prettily. The Dr think it very becoming but I suppose it will soon be out of fashion now I come into it, but I don't give myself much trouble about it, for I have it done but once a week. Every Saturday my maid do it up with water and it holds in curl all the week. Mrs Browne's maid desired the ends of the hair might be just snipped every time it was done up and she said it would make my hair grow strong and thick all over which I find it does better than anything I ever tried.

The Dr has got a new music book from Cambridge lately published, that cost half a guinea. The tunes are set as well as any master can set them. I have got 3 of the songs, one is to a very pretty minuet that Mrs Houghton played here. I practice a great deal now.

From Elizabeth Postlethwaite
Denton, 12 November 1742

My Dear Sister,

I received the Dr's letter on Sunday, which I take very kindly. I am so bad a writer I dursn't write to him again, but most heartily wish him and you, joy of your little daughter and am much pleased to hear you are both in so good a way, which I pray God continue.

I think my mother seem pleased you have made it of her name, I shall very willingly oblige you in being Godmother to my little niece, or anything else that is in my power.[83] I have made her a pair of shoes, my mother gave me the silk. You must bid her be tidy of them or else I shall whip her when I come. They are to be sent to London to the Bishop's that they may cost nothing the coming. Pray remember me to nurse, and tell her I want to be her assistant very much.

83. The Bishop of Norwich had agreed to be Tilly's Godfather. Mrs Postlethwaite and Elizabeth asked Samuel Kerrich 'to lay out 50 shillings...one guinea of which they would have given to the midwife, another guinea to the nurse and the remainder to the 3 servants. And if you have 2 nurses, they would have you bestow a guinea on the second nurse and they will be accounted to you for that': Ms 591, f. 130 Mathew Postlethwaite to Samuel Kerrich, 10 Dec. 1742.

The Duet (1749)
Oil painting by Arthur Devis
By courtesy of the V & A Picture Library

From Elizabeth Postlethwaite
Denton, 23 December 1742

Dear Sister,

You can't imagine the pleasure it give me to hear your dear little girl thrives so finely and is so likely to live, and that you are able to be so good a nurse. I didn't think you would have been strong enough to have suckled it, but am afraid it should be too much for you a nights if she should grow tedious.

I am impatient to see her, and then you say she is like me, I hope you won't think a journey to Denton too far for her this Summer, for I must see her. I will borrow a cradle for her and my room will make a good nursery. What do little Johnny think of her? I suppose he rock her sometimes. Mrs Smith our neighbour have buried her son Ames,[84] which is a great sorrow to her. He was her favourite, she thought him so like Mr Smith. I have nothing of news to tell you. We all join with respects and the good wishes of the season. I thank God I hold pretty well.

From Barbara Kerrich
Dersingham, 2 January 1743

Dear Sister,

I received your kind and affectionate letter to myself and little girl and I shall be glad to have her able to make a visit at Denton this Summer, if it please God she go on with thriving as she does at present, I dare say she will.

My mother very kindly invited her in both her letters to me, but I wrote in such haste last time I quite forgot to thank her for it, which I hope you will do for me. Sarah's milk agree with the child, she looks with a mighty healthful clear complexion. Johnny says she is a pretty rogue enough, but he often tells us, he hopes we won't turn him away because we should have a boy and a girl. He says he don't love rocking for he can't stand still. He is going into breeches, for he has torn all his frocks[85] off his back, and is in great haste to have the breeches made. Just now he came into the parlour with his brother Martin's boots on

---

84. Ames Smith died 23 November 1742, the 4th surviving child of Ames Smith (1702-1738) and Sarah, daughter of Robert Tite, Gent: Blomefield, V, p. 412.

85. Boys generally gave up wearing frocks and began to dress like their fathers at the age of three or four, girls like their mothers from the age of two: L. Stone, op. cit., p. 258.

and all his petticoats but his under one turned up and tied about his neck, and said he should give away his shoes and wear only boots now. I am heartily glad to hear that you hold so well this Winter and wish you many happy years.

From Elizabeth Postlethwaite
Denton, 15 June 1743

Dear Sister,

I hope the Dr have quite got the better of his distemper, for Mr Brock say he seem brisk and well, and I hope you are in a way to increase your family because you sent your jumps[86] to be altered, but your ordering them to be lessened that made me I don't know what to think of it, but you will let me know when you write.

Though I thank God I am much stronger and better than ever I was since I have been ill, I dare not set my heart too much upon the thoughts of ever being well enough to meet at Dersingham, though there is nothing in the world would be a greater pleasure to me than being often together, and Tilly is such a pretty rogue that her innocent prattle would be always diverting. Tell her she is a good girl to send her duty, and I pray God bless her and preserve her life.

My mother wrote to my cousin Johnson this week to find the Dereham carrier and bid him get you a stone of soap and pay for it. I suppose we may send our letters by him as well as by the post, if she can find him out. I am very glad you like the bargain, for a silk gown is useless for me, I will send it by Mr Brock and get the calico as you desire I should. The present I sent Tilly is not worth a thank, but I thought if you liked to make her a silk coat, there would be enough now she is so little.

Mrs Smith of Harleston and three of her children are gone to Bedfordshire. I believe she had a mind to have one quarrel more with Mr Ralph about the chapel window[87] before they parted, for she sent her son Charles to chapel on Whitsunday. Prayers were begun when he came in, he shut the window as soon as he came in. Mr Ralph ordered it to be opened; he shut it a second time. Then Mr Ralph ordered the churchwarden to turn him out, so the gentleman was

86. 'A sort of bodice for a woman': Bailey.

87 The chapel dedicated to St John the Baptist, was rebuilt in 1726 at a cost of £1100, £700 of which was raised locally: Harleston was at this time part of the parish of Redenhall: Blomefield, V, pp. 356-357.

obliged to walk off. It made great confusion and you see something of Mr Ralph's fiery temper when you were at Denton. He have lost all favour at Harleston, he have behaved oddly in a great many respects. He court Miss Langley, Mrs Paston have endeavoured to break it off, but it's thought they carry it on privately. She is at London and one of her sisters, they went to buy new clothes. Mr and Mrs Farrow were at Mr Dalling's on Sunday, they left the two children and a maid. I suppose they will stay most part of the Summer.

The Bishop have sent the chariot. If he had got it new painted, it would have look like a new one, it's lined with red. My mother have sent it today for Mrs Arrowsmith and Mrs Ellis[88] to dine here.

From Barbara Kerrich
Dersingham, 13 February 1744

Dear Sister,

I just write a line or two to let you know I am got quite well again, for which I have great reason to bless God, for the child I dare say had been dead a good while. I was but poorly sometime before, but was loath to complain, because I knew I should be blamed for want of care of myself, and I did expect what would happen. I did not take my drink neither, and the Dr being so ill, I didn't think much about myself. I hope he is a great deal better, but he has still everyday a slight return of the fever notwithstanding he goes on in the method my brother advised him to as near as he can.

I thank God my little girl grow finely and is more and more like your picture every day, only her hair is a very light brown. Strangers can see the likeness and she surprise everybody with her talking, she speak so plain, and almost every word she hear, and know the meaning of some words. For when she want to drink she say, 'I dry,' and when 'tis night she say, 'dark, dark,' and can call everybody in the house by their names, and when she have a mind to go to Sarah's, she say 'Nurse, nurse, see boys,' and there she is as jolly as any of them, and trot about, for she begin to walk prettily with only holding her back string ever since Sarah's christening. When she go there, she call

88. Less than a month after Mr Cremer's rejection, Sukey Arrowsmith unexpectedly married a Mr Ellis, possibly the Reverend Robert Ellis, a member of the Bungay Gentlemen's Club (1745). On this occasion £400 of her fortune was settled on her, Mathew Postlethwaite being one of the trustees: Ethel Mann, *Old Bungay* (1934), p. 170; Ms 588, f. 168 Matilda Postlethwaite to Barbara Kerrich, 15 Jan. 1742.

out 'dance, dance,' and take hold of her frock of each side and jig about. One of the young men that were at Sarah's could play upon the violin, so Molly and Sarah's sister and some more made up four couple and Sarah danced with Tilly in her arms that the child was so delighted she wouldn't come home till nine o'clock, that she was just asleep, and then she kept talking of dancing. She has cut two double teeth more, but no eye teeth yet, and them I fear most.

Pray don't forget to send Mrs Houghton's bottle of cordial water next time anybody come this way. Mr Hammond Mrs Hoste's father, died last Thursday. I talked of writing a line or two when I began, but should have said a side or two.

From Barbara Kerrich
Dersingham, 24 April 1744.

Dear Sister,

I am going to write a letter to you, which I believe will be all confusion, between the desire I have of seeing you and of showing you my dear little girl, and the fear I have of her health.

Mrs Gregson is just come home from seeing her friends at Norwich and Attleborough, and brought such dismal accounts of sickness everywhere that have disconcerted all our schemes. She says at Norwich in particular there is a very bad fever and measles besides the smallpox, and that so bad that she left Mr Gregson at Attleborough and only went to Norwich herself, he having never had the smallpox, and in the country towns she passed through, people airing themselves that looked very fresh got up of the smallpox, and in one place no less than three feather beds laid in a yard close by the roadside where it was known the smallpox had very lately been, that she says she has been in continual fear. We observed the bill of mortality either last week or the week before was increased 26 in one week at Norwich. It is very sickly hereabouts too, at Lynn there is an exceeding bad fever and very mortal. When you see my cousin Johnson you will be able to give us a true, and I hope a better account from Norwich. Everybody here discourage us very much.

We have been at Mr Gregson's this afternoon and there was more company, and we were talking of our journey, and one of the ladies said if we had half dozen children she thought we might venture to carry one abroad this sickly season, but as it was, she thought it would not bear any dispute. Tilly was with us and merry as a cricket, crowing and laughing and looking of everybody and everything, you would be surprised to see how she rejoice at tea things, not that she'll drink much, but she love to put her hands among them and see the tea poured out. But if she hears anybody turn over the leaves of a book she is ready to fly off one's lap, there's nothing please her, nor quiet her if she be crying, so soon, as giving her a book to turn over the leaves, which she will do herself very prettily. I thank God she has fine health and I wish you could see her. I have got all her short coats made and six new white frocks thinking we should have set out this week, but we must stay till we hear the country is more healthful. I can't say I am right well myself, but shall be glad to hear you are.

From Elizabeth Postlethwaite
Denton, 1 March 1745

Dear Sister,

I thank you for the pleasure you express at the thoughts of seeing me this Summer, but though I thank God I am much stronger and better than I have been ever since I kept my chamber, I shan't be able to take such a journey this year. I shall be glad if I can next. I wish Tilly were near enough that she and Johnny might come everyday to see me, it would be the greatest pleasure in the world to me, but I see her almost every night in my sleep, there have been but few nights but what I have dreamt of her since she was here.

We are like to have a toping neighbour at that house that was Mr Dalling's. Sir John Playter's son[89] is about buying of it, and if Mrs Suckling and he can agree for it, he talk of coming to live here at a Lady.[90] Miss Jacombe is married to Mr Kitty Barry, it is a very great match for him, her uncle Acton left her 4000 pound. My cousin Johnson's daughter now lie in and is very weak, and she have got so bad a husband that she want necessaries. I am so cold I can write no more.

89. Probably John Playters of Yelverton, husband of Anne Caroline, daughter and co-heir of Sir John Turner (1712-1780), 2nd Baronet of Wareham: W. Rye, op. cit., p.679, G.E.C. I, pp. 220-221.

90. Lady Day, the Feast of the Annunciation, 25th March: Harvey, p. 457.

From Elizabeth Postlethwaite
Denton, 8 August 1745

Dear Sister,

I am very glad you found little Tilly so well, and that she was easy the time you were here and that you had a good journey. I wish I could fix a time for mine, everything is so uncertain as to my brother, that I can't determine anything about myself till I see how he will be settled, but he have wrote to Oxford as the Dr advise him, that I hope it won't be long before we shall know how things will be.[91]

My mother send my cousin Johnson to Norwich tomorrow to buy some things for her, and she is to look of the landau, and if they will take one of the seats out I dare say a bed will lie very well, and the motion will be easier for me than anything I can have. I shall like it much better to come so then, anyway.

My brother have given me all the things that are in my room. My mother will go away next week,[92] I can't prevail with her to stay any longer, but I will keep my cousin Johnson here as long as I stay. She will be some company for me for I can't bear to be without somebody. Mr and Mrs Fairman dined here today. My mother made her a present of some of her things I dare say, for there was a bundle put into the chariot. I thank you for sending your gown, it will do better than any gown I have for the journey.

From Elizabeth Postlethwaite
Denton, 13 September 1745

Dear Sister,

I received the letters and the things on Sunday, my cousin Johnson give you thanks for them. She say she shall mend them and make them last a good while, but she heard last week that the child was like to die - it would be a good thing if it do.

91. Presumably he wrote to Merton College, Oxford on the death of Mathew Postlethwaite, to make a case for succeeding his father as Rector of Denton. The Archbishop of Canterbury was perpetual patron of the living, but was obliged 'to present, such persons as shall be...or have been (formerly fellows) of Merton College in Oxford' under the conditions of John Postlethwaite's will dated 5th September 1713. John Postlethwaite had purchased the advowson of Denton from the Duke of Norfolk: Blomefield, V, p. 412 n.3.

92. On her husband's death, Matilda Postlethwaite moved to Benacre, where she died in 1760.

My mother have been very bad since I wrote to you, her stomach quite gone, that it was a punishment to her to get anything down. She is trying chocolate in a morning and take some mutton broth in an afternoon, for she think kitchen physic is best for her. We sent Tom on Wednesday to know how she did, and she is something better, I doubt she will hardly live long. My brother have had a fever but has got finely to what he was, it hath made him weak and faint.

Nan go to be cook at Benacre that I don't know what we are to do, though here have been one to let herself, but I can only hire her by the week as things are so uncertain. The Bishop have got a living worth a 170 pound a year for a change for my brother, but he is not willing to change till he see whether he can have this. When you write don't mention anything that I have told you of it.

Mrs Stone is a very fine bride, she have two suits of clothes, her best are a silver tissue[93] trimmed with gold and three gold flounces upon the petticoat: her other suit is a white satin. She have a pair of diamond earrings cost 200 pound and a handsome laced head. Her night gown is a white flowered with silver and is very fine too. My brother have sent the Dr and you, each of you, a ring and hope the Dr excuse his not writing now. He will write by Mr Brock and send the book he promised. My mother left Tilly these boxes to play with when she went away.

From Elizabeth Postlethwaite
Denton, 4 October 1745

Dear Sister,

I am very glad to hear you are all well. Goodman Shimon frightened me by telling me the danger the Dr was in when the horses run away, he had a very narrow escape.

Tilly's purging will do her good now she is cutting teeth I hope. My brother have not heard from Oxford yet, that I don't know when we shall be settled. He bid me tell you he would have answered the Dr's letter before now, but he had a particular reason that have hindered him. I have hired a maid, she have the character of a sober honest body and good tempered. She have never lived but in a farmer's house, but I thought she might do for us.

We had Mr and Mrs Stillingfleet dined with us on Tuesday. Little

93. 'Rich stuff made of silk, silver or gold woven together': Bailey.

Miss Barry is like to get well though they are afraid she will be lame. Miss Langley is married to a gentleman from London. It's thought a sorry match for her but Mrs Paston say he will be worth in a few years a great many thousand pounds. I have had Mrs Smith of Harleston to see me twice. She brought her sister Peggy with her from Bedfordshire, but she didn't come with her to see me.

My cousin Johnson went to Norwich last week but she come to me again Monday or Tuesday. She is to get you a wash ball and send by the Dereham carrier. I often wonder I hold so well, I ought to be very thankful for it and take it as a great mercy, I couldn't have thought I should have held so well, for it is the greatest affliction I ever met with. I shall never have any pleasure again in Denton, that I wish with all my heart my brother would take Melton.[94] Goody Shimon hasn't been to see me yet, I wonder at it for I should like to see her and talk with her. Tell Tilly I want her to divert me and to talk of the Pretender.[95]

From Barbara Kerrich
Dersingham, 10 December 1745

Dear Sister,

I write to you now in the greatest confusion as is all the country hereabouts, for yesterday it was reported that the rebels would be at Lynn as tomorrow, but we had a letter from Dr Pyle[96] just now, and he says the rebels are at Ashbourne in Derbyshire, the Duke[97] at Coventry and Marshal Wade[98] at Mansfield, this is the last advice. However, he says we are greatly alarmed. The rebels, may some of them straggle hither if thrashed, or the French may come, who are making a vast embarkation. We are arming to defend ourselves and if we hear they bend this way, we shall cut down all our bridges and lay ships in the shallower parts to defend us. This is what was in Dr Pyle's letter.

94. Melton Constable.

95. Charles Edward Stuart (1720-1788), the Young Pretender: Harvey, p. 663.

96. Edmund Pyle (fl. 1720-1776), succeeded father Thomas Pyle as Lecturer at St. Nicholas Lynn 1732; Chaplain to the King 1738-1776. He was a close friend of both Mathew Postlethwaite and Samuel Kerrich: Venn, III, p. 410.

97. William Augustus, Duke of Cumberland (1721-1765), 3rd son of George II and Commander of the English army at Culloden: Harvey, p. 208.

98. George Wade (1673-1748), Commander-in-Chief of the English army in 1745, but superseded for failing to stop the advance of the rebels: Harvey, p. 865.

This is a little respite, but God know what is to become of us, nor where we can go, for to be sure, they will be all over the county if they come here. We have packed up our most valuable things to hide somewhere if they do come. Mrs Gregson and we meet almost every day to contrive and comfort one another. I pray God you may be safe where you are. I don't know where to wish you for the best and that we may meet again in this world. Tilly that was one of my greatest pleasures is now my greatest sorrow when I look upon her, to think of what may befall her. She never was so well and looks like the picture of health and grow very tall. Pray God preserve her.

Pray desire Mr Baldry to send the money without fail by Mr Brock who said he would come at Christmas, for we have paid away all our money in expectation of that, and here is no money to be had here now, that we must have it. God grant us a meeting in better times. I wrote to my mother 6 weeks ago and have had no answer, that I doubt it miscarried.

From Barbara Kerrich
Dersingham, 17 December 1745

Dear Sister,

I give you a great many thanks for your kind present of the edging. I am quite ashamed of taking so many things as you are so kind to give us, and I never have anything for you, unless it be a little old holland. I have some of that now, but don't know whether you want it because I think you have some, but if it will be of any service to you I will send it by Mr Brock when he come at Candlemas.[99]

'Tis 12 o'clock and I write in a great hurry, we have been at Houghton today. It proved a fine morning, and the Dr make me take all opportunities of going out now because he thinks it is good for me, and I dare say it obliged Mr Baldry highly, for they wouldn't have seen anything without us that signify, and they saw everything and tasted of the Hogan.[100] Tilly was so merry and comical there, she made everybody laugh. She did run and fly about, and the housekeeper got her and laid her onto the velvet bed,[101] and kissed her and was mightily pleased with her.

99. Candlemas, the Festival of the Purification of the Blessed Virgin Mary, 2nd February: Harvey p. 139.
100. Houghton was famous for its ale, known as hogan.
101. Perhaps the bed made by William Kent for the Green Velvet Bedchamber.

Benacre Hall, Suffolk (1824)
Engraved from a painting by Henry Davy
By courtesy of the Suffolk Record Office, Ipswich Adm 1/10/KALC

Houghton in Norfolk, the seat of the Earl of Orford (1779)
Drawn and engraved by William Watts
By courtesy of the Witt Library, Courtauld Institute, London

The Dr have not yet had Mr Sayer's bill of the lease, or would have sent you the money for the gown. I suppose my brother will show you what the Dr has said about Frank Baldry in his letter.

From Elizabeth Postlethwaite
Denton, 26 December 1745

Dear Sister,

I received your letter with a good deal of concern. I was in fears for you before, for it was reported here that the rebels were expected at Lynn everyday. I wished you all here, I thought perhaps you might be safer here as we have but few houses hereabouts to what you have worth plundering, that it's possible they may escape us. I should wish to be all together if it should please God to suffer such a dreadful thing to happen, but I hope God Almighty will defend and keep us. Our apprehension and fears I hope will prove greater than our sufferings. There is some good news in the papers this week, that I hope God will fight for us and we shall be safe.

Mr Baldry paid the money to me. I didn't know Mr Brock designed being at Dersingham so soon, that made my brother think of getting the money returned to Lynn because we didn't know which way to get it to you. My brother is not at well a days and is very thin; he look sadly, he lay things very much to heart. I believe you guess the reason right that Mr Baldry didn't come. My brother is gone to see my mother, I had a letter from her about a week ago, she tell me she have quite lost her stomach again, her constitution is quite broke. I doubt, I am afraid, she will never have her health again. I hope God Almighty will preserve and keep dear Tilly from all harm, however it shall please Him to order things.

From Barbara Kerrich
Dersingham, 7 January 1746

Dear Sister,

I wrote to you last week, I thank God I hold pretty well. I am glad Mr Baldry was so well pleased. Tilly was very comical all the time they were here, she don't mind peoples being strangers to her now, but she go on in her own way.

Poor Tabby's little boy died that day Mr Baldry went from hence, he had had the measles and I fancy got cold, and she didn't purge him after it, but the child was quite choked up. Tabby quite vapoured me when she came, she is so concerned she is big with child again. Tomorrow the Doctor is invited to attend the corpse of poor Mr Styleman[102] who died yesterday of the numb palsy, his son that was at Bungay is worse than ever.

The Dr say the sum due to you from Frank Baldry is one and twenty pound and six shillings. The six shillings he gave him back, and told him he imagined you would do the same. My brother is to pay you 5 pound a part of the six pound 15 that was due to you from the Dr last Michaelmas. I quite forgot to desire Mr Baldry to pay for the sassafras.[103]

From Elizabeth Postlethwaite
Denton, 1 February 1746

Dear Sister,

I have waited so long for Mr Brock that I am afraid you will think me negligent in writing. I have sent Mr Baldry's money by him, there is 12 pound two shillings and threepence. The Dr will see by the bills there is an odd two pence halfpenny. Mr Baldry asked to have sixpence returned for that.

I think my brother now fixed to be happy having got the place he so much wished for, and I hope he will be so when all his affairs are settled. Mr Nicholls[104] was here a week, he is a most obliging, good natured worthy man, my brother could not have met with such another. I believe he intend to return to Portugal as soon as he can. He had a Portuguese servant with him, he couldn't speak a word of English.

I have never told you of poor Mrs Ellis's misfortune, for her husband was arrested sometime ago for a debt of 30 pound that Mrs Arrowsmith is bound for, but it brought all the rest of his creditors upon him that he must be ruined. He is gone off, there are bailiffs now

102. Nicholas Styleman Esq of Snettisham, married to Armine, daughter of Sir Nicholas L'Estrange, 3rd Baronet, died 6 Jan. 1746. Their third son, Robert Styleman 'died an imbecile', date unknown: Venn IV, pp. 182, 183; Elizabeth M. James, 'The Old Hall, Snettisham And The Styleman Family,' *Norfolk Archaeology* XXXVIII (1983), pp. 343-357.

103. Sassafras, 'the bark and root of a tree growing in America, which have an aromatic smell and taste, and are much used in physic': Bailey.

104. John Nicholls (b.1706), Resident Chaplain to the merchants at Oporto; Rector of Redenhall 1745-1748: Blomefield, V, p. 361; Venn, III, p. 255

at his house. It is very hard for her and she is not able to bear misfortunes as some people are, that doubt it will soon break her heart.

I am very sorry to hear dear Tilly have got an ague, but as Spring is coming on I hope it won't hold her long. I have sent her a little pack of cards my brother happened on, he thought they would please her. I shall be impatient for Mr Brock's return to know how she do.

I have got six yards of white calico for a gown, but I was forced to give four and sixpence a yard for the man I bought it on had none besides this but what was too coarse. I hear Ruth Brady is come from Dersingham. She have got a farmer's service in the town but I suppose she won't stay long, for it is but a sorry place.

From Barbara Kerrich
Dersingham, 25 February 1746

Dear Sister,

I am sorry you have been so much out of order and should have wrote last week, but expected Mr Brock would have come the beginning of this, and hoped I should have sent you something for a martage. But the week after your last letter came, the weather proved so very bad that the person that I employed to buy it couldn't go till the Saturday when the mart people had all packed up, but I will get it as soon as I can. I would have got a cream boat or a neat cream pot, but there was none to be had in the town of Lynn but great clumsy things.

I should have got Tilly a martage too, but it was too late, for Mrs Houghton was so kind to desire me to lay out the six shillings (at the mart for a plaything) which Miss Browne owed her ever since she was here, and I got it for her a little while ago. Mrs Gregson didn't go for fear of the measles, or else we should have got everything. Tilly had a little present from the mart,[105] a neat set of white stone tea things fit for her little teapot that my brother sent her. The newsman is come that I must not write any more. Frank Baldry has the receipt that the Dr signed for his part and you are to sign the same.

105. Lynn Mart, the annual fair took place on 2nd February. There were also weekly markets on Tuesday and Saturday. In the seventeenth century the potters' stalls were on the north side of the Market Cross together with the iron merchants and nailmakers: Vanessa Parker, *The Making of King's Lynn* (Chichester 1971), pp. 45, 127-128.

The Tuesday Market Place, King's Lynn
Engraving of a drawing by Henry Bell (died 1717)
By courtesy of King's Lynn Library

From Elizabeth Postlethwaite
Denton, 19 April 1746

Dear Sister,

I have got Miss Jenny Kerrich with me, she came to see me and my brother asked her to stay with me a little while, and she and I were very busy yesterday in putting up this little lady that my brother bought Tilly at London. She is a dancer, but she ought to carry her dancing master with her, for I don't know very well how to direct you to teach her. You are to set her upon a table and somebody should beat a tune to her with their fists upon the table and that will make her move about. I fancy Tilly will be pleased with her, I suppose she will be for making all her babies dance. She lost one of her eyes in coming home, I put a drop of ink in. I hope she won't be broke, I desired Mr Brock to take care of her. My brother tell me he have invited you to come with the Dr, don't come without Tilly, for I want to see her very much. I should be glad to hear by Mr Brock when you can fix the time for coming.

Poor Mr Dalling have managed so that he have sold that pretty house they now live in. It have been gone sometime but I have never thought to mention it till now. I am vexed for him, it is very well that he can't spend the other estate, for I am afraid that would go too if it were in his power. I heard this week that poor Nan that lived here is dead of the smallpox at Mr Gooch's. She went there at Michaelmas.

From Barbara Kerrich
Dersingham, 21 April 1746

Dear Sister,

The reason you hadn't my last letter sooner was because the Dereham carrier was ill and did not come of a fortnight, that I was forced to send it by the post at last, but he is got better and brought yours.

I am very much concerned to find you have been so much out of order, but I hope it is owing in a great measure to the unseasonableness of the Spring, for I think a colder April never was felt. I shall be impatient to hear that you have recovered this disorder, which I hope I shall as the weather grow warmer. I wonder we haven't seen Mr Brock, he promised to be here the last week in March.

I thank God Tilly continue finely brisk and well and order her babies so comically she often make me laugh. The baby she call Sally is often whipped for her cap being off, but t'other day 'twas only a little o' one side. 'Aye,' says she, 'now 'tis only slipshod I shan't whip you, but when 'tis quite off I always will.' The Dr wonder he does not hear from my brother.

I had just finished this letter when Mr Brock came to send it by the carrier. You seem to write with good spirits and I hope you are better. I am glad Miss Jenny is with you, I think she is pretty company now you are so much alone.

The little lady came very safe. I think it is the prettiest thing I ever saw, she look quite genteel; we are very much obliged to my brother for it. Tilly is highly pleased with it, she said, 'what shall I do for my uncle? I have a good mind to go and see him one day'. And she saw me smile and she nodded her head and said, 'nay, I will indeed.' We make her dance, but I don't know whether right, for they need have good hard hands that do it.

I am vexed for poor Nan. I had a letter from my mother last week, and she told me that one of Mr Gooch's servants fell down of the smallpox soon after they came home, and that was three more that had not had it, and they were in great fears for master. As my brother have given us so kind an invitation we shall let you know soon what time we can conveniently come, if the smallpox be not at Norwich nor thereabouts.

From Barbara Kerrich
Dersingham, 19 August 1746?

Dear Sister,

I hope you hold as well as when I left you as you said nothing to the contrary, and I think it very good and kind in you to stay to take care of my brother's household affairs, but still you must consider your own health a little, and unless you could be assured that my brother and you could stay and keep house there all the Winter, it will soon be time for you to think of coming before the days grow short and cold, and if my brother like the scheme we were talking on of Miss Jenny Kerrich, I should think that would do.

We are in a little hopes of hearing of a horse litter, for about a month ago here was one came somewhere near Raynham, carried by two large mules, with a sick or ancient person from London, and if it be possible we'll make out where they had it and what the charge.[106]It went to Toftrees, I think the town's name is, to a clergyman's. That certainly will be safest for you, for if a wheel carriage go ever so softly over rough roads the motion is very shaking. I design to get Mr Utber to go to Toftrees and inquire about it and then I will let you know.

Mrs Hayward is now at Mr Gregson's and go away the beginning of next week and as you desired, I will send a few old things to my cousin Johnson's of Tilly's, by her, so you may send for them on Saturday sennight to Mr Hayward's, because they will be directed to you. They are hardly worth sending for, but my cousin Johnson love mending and you said she would like any old thing better than nothing. I wish my cousin would take care that the Dereham carrier might always have your letters, for your last letter did not come by him, and I hadn't it till the day after he was here. He say my cousin Johnson know where he set up, but he didn't see any of them last week.

From Barbara Kerrich
Dersingham, Holy Rood day, 14 September 1746?

Dear Sister,

This being your birthday, I wish and heartily pray it may bring you new joy and health, and that you may see many of <u>them</u> <u>so</u>, which would make both yourself and friends rejoice.

I am very much concerned to hear you have been so bad, but Charles says in his letter, he hopes you are gathering strength again. I have sent you a bed gown, I had just enough, mine was forced to be pieced[107] as much as this, the stitching was so sadly cut and spoiled when my clothes were made, but I think the brimstone spots are spread more with lying up, since my gown was done. I and Sarah made it, as we did mine, by one of Mrs Hoste's. I wish you may like it, but am afraid the sleeve is rather too short for you. The calico should have come down a little longer, but I had hardly enough of that.

Here's a few feathers, I was in hopes I should have got more, if you like the turkey cocks feathers, you may have more of them. My

106. Two years later it cost 36 shillings a day to hire a horse litter in London. The maximum distance covered in a day was 20 miles by this method of travel: Ms 586, f.223 Matilda Postlethwaite to Barbara Kerrich, 18 Dec. 1748.

107. Made up of several pieces of material.

poor shell duck is dead, it was starved. We turned them out of the garden in the Spring because we thought they ate the young lettuces and things, and I believe the other fowls beat her that she couldn't get enough to keep her alive. The drake is a fine creature still; he is put into the garden. I had the duck stuffed in order to send you, but we didn't think of the head, and that stank so in a week, we were forced to throw feathers and all away. We are going to dinner and shall drink your health.

From Elizabeth Postlethwaite
Denton, 4 December 1746

Dear Sister,

I am sorry to hear you have had a return of the toothache, I wish you would let me persuade you to try claret and myrrh, nothing ever did me so much good as that. I know you hate the taste of it, but the worst taste in the world is better than pain of the teeth. I never had pain of the teeth very bad since I used it.

I am mighty glad Tilly is so finely well. Mr Kerrich was here this week, he said he had given you directions about purging her. He brought two of the Dr's sermons. I have read it and like it and return him my thanks for it, and also for the trouble he have had in writing to Mr Sayer.[108] What reason Mr Sayer can have that he is not willing to write this codicil into my will I can't imagine, though I think, I can't well make any mistake, but as to disobliging my brother; he will never know nothing of the matter. Mr Kerrich told me that the Dr thought it would be better to let Mr Sayer see my will, so I desired him to carry it.[109] Miss Long must make a most sad figure amongst so many fine clothes and fine ladies. Her dress, I think, was fitter for a masquerade than an assembly. She used to be odd and whimsical I think.

108. Daniel Sayer, attorney, of Harleston was a younger son of Thomas Sayer: Blomefield, V, p. 401.

109. Spinsters and widows could own and freely dispose of property; the situation for married women was far more complex: A. Laurence, op. cit., pp. 228-230.

From Elizabeth Postlethwayt
Denton, 4 February 1747

Dear Sister,

You had had a letter from me last week, but that I forgot that the market at Norwich was to be kept on the Friday, that when I sent my letter and Mr Kerrich's, the man that should have carried them was gone. I am glad you are got well and that you intend to try tar water,[110] I hope that will keep you so.

Mr Baldry paid me last week my part of the rent of Frank Baldry's farm. I had in money only six pound 8 shillings and 7 pence, but he said there was 50 shillings more due to me, which by mistake the Dr took off his son. Mr Barry is High Sheriff for Suffolk, my brother dined with him at the Book Club[111] on Tuesday, and with Mr Stillingfleet his Chaplain. Old Mrs Suckling is dead. She lay a long time ill, Mrs Baldry was with her a month I believe, before she died. She had only under bearers, they had hatbands and gloves, and each of them a guinea. Mr Baldry was one of the bearers.

I didn't expect to hear you would ever be a knitter, it was a work I thought you never liked. You will outdo me, I knit so slow it make me weary of it, I haven't done any a long time. I have read Mrs Davys's[112] books through, I am very well pleased with them, they have diverted me several hours. I think *The Reformed Coquet* is very pretty. I must go and write a short epistle to poor Tilly , and to my cousin Johnson I must write. Mrs Rackham was here almost all last week, she desired her duty.

---

110. Tar water, popularised by George, Bishop Berkeley (1685-1753), was believed to be a remedy for various disorders including colic. Elizabeth Postlethwaite had previously recommended it for Samuel Kerrich: Harvey, p. 84; Buchan, p. 300; Ms 589 f. 47, Elizabeth Postlethwaite to Barbara Kerrich, 16 Nov. 1744.

111. There was a book club at Beccles, active in the 1770s with 42 members paying a subscription of one guinea a year: Michael Ellwood, 'Library Provision In A Small Market Town, 1700-1929,' *Library History* V (1979), pp. 50-51.

112. Mary Davys (1674-1732), novelist and playwright, who established a coffee house at Cambridge. *The Reformed Coquet* (1724) was immensely popular, numbering Pope and Gay among the subscribers. The sisters equally enjoyed her play *The Self Rival.* Janet Todd (ed.), *Dictionary of British Women Writers* (1989), pp. 179-181.

From Barbara Kerrich
Dersingham, 19 March 1747

Dear Sister,

To make amends for not writing to you last week, you will receive two letters from me this, for after Monday was over I didn't expect Mr Brock, but wrote o'Tuesday by the newsman, and Mr Brock came two or three hours after I had sent it away.

I am mightily pleased with the book you sent me, I believe I looked on it every day all the time I was at Denton. You can't imagine how those old sayings and signs take my fancy. I should have asked for it then, but that I thought it wasn't yours. The minute I saw the book before I read your letter, I thought of what Lady Davers says to Mrs B. You never forget the smallest things that are kind and obliging, for I thought you sent it because you remember how I used to study it over. The recipe I shall certainly try, and nettles will soon be in perfection, which you know used to be reckoned excellent things in the Spring. I thank God I have had nothing of that disorder since, nor never before, that sometimes I flatter myself it might possibly be occasioned by my being a breeding, though I never heard of anybody that bred with such a symptom, but to be sure I was a breeding then though I didn't know it.

I wish I was within twenty mile of you and I would make you a visit now you are alone. I am glad my brother was so good to think of somebody to keep you company whilst he is gone, though you have almost as much need on it when he is at home, but however it was kindly said. Give our service to Mrs Ellis and to Mr Blyford. I am glad you approve of what I design to get for you. I have made a smart cap and pinner of that edging you sent me with the edging of Tilly's muffetees[113] that you gave her. I hadn't enough without it; I like it as well as anything I have to my head.

The Dr is as busy as a bee looking after the stopping up the windows in this great rambling house.[114] We shall pay for above forty

113. Worsted cuffs worn on the wrists.
114. The Window tax, 'An Act For Granting To His Majesty Several Rates Or Dues Upon Houses For Making Good The Deficiency Of The Clipped Money 7 & 8 Gul.III, cap.18 (1695)', was levied upon the occupants of houses with more than a certain number of windows, particularly resented by those living in larger properties. It was frequently revised during the Georgian period, lastly in 1808: John Burke (ed.), *Jowett's Dictionary of English Law* (2v., 1977), 2, p. 1906.

do what we can, but paying for the chariot disturb me more by half.[115] 'Tis a sad thing to pay for going abroad and staying at home too, if we have any light. The Dr says you forgot to date the receipts.

From Elizabeth Postlethwaite
Denton, 16 April 1747

Dear Sister,

I have sent you a cleansing cloth and cheese cloth, but I had no opportunity of sending to Mr Brock for them, so I got them of Mr Wright as they are things of so small a value I thought it didn't signify, for my brother never like I should send his man anywhere.

I had a letter from my mother this week. She mentioned her sending Tilly the riddle upon the vowels, and was so well pleased with your answer that she wished for another to send you. The riddle and answer are both gone to Bungay for Mrs Ellis was highly pleased with them too and wrote them out. She left me that week I wrote to you last. Mr Kerrich sent his two daughters to make me a visit the time my brother was at London. Miss Sukey I think is a fine girl, she grow very like her mama.

Mrs Stone was brought to bed of a son last week. That family and Mr Parsons[116] have had a very great quarrel. Mr Stone[117] one Sunday when it rained, would have had his coach been driven up to the church door; Mr Parsons would not let it. Mr Stone have given him warning to leave his house and Mr Parsons is a going to live in his other parish, he is about buying a house there. There is several little quarrels between them. Mr Parsons sometime ago preached a sermon against pride which Mrs Stone took very ill.

I must tell you before I conclude that I have been abroad. You will think me very venturous, or the Dr will I am sure, but those few fine days we had the beginning of April were so tempting I couldn't forbear, and I catched no cold.

115. Act 20 Geo II, cap. 4 (1747), exacted an excise duty on carriages, 'a yearly sum of four pounds for every coach, Berlin, Landau, Calash with four wheels, Chaise Marine, Chaise with four wheels and Caravan, or by what means soever such Carriages now are or hereafter may be called or known': G. Eland (ed.), op. cit., I, p. 179-180. Samuel Kerrich owned a landau.

116. Joseph Parsons (1698-1774), Rector of Hempnall 1724 and Vicar of Bedingham 1725-1774: Foster (Early Series), III, p. 1123.

117. William Stone, Esq of Bedingham (d. 1 March 1762): G.M. XXXII (1762), p. 145.

The riddle upon the vowels

Mama and I have tried our wits
To find these little airy chits.
We guessed and then she had me look
I found the vowels in my book.
She bid me mind how they were set:
One in glass and one in jet.
In tin, in box, and one in you
These often am, and set to view.
But my head runs of other things,
So away they fly as if they had wings.[118]

**From Elizabeth Postlethwaite
Denton, 16 June 1747**

Dear Sister,

You will see I designed sending this other letter by the carrier for I didn't know of Mr Brock's setting out tomorrow, till I was a going to send my letter away to Norwich.

I have seen my father's picture, but it was not quite finished.[119] There was a little matter to do to the drapery and to frame, that it was obliged to go back again. I want very much you should see it, I am vastly pleased with it, I think I never see so great a likeness in any picture in my life.[120] Mrs Farrow have buried her eldest little girl of the smallpox, and one of her other now lie of it very bad. Old Mrs Farrow is dead, she died very suddenly.

The cook maid that came here last Michaelmas, just before she came she was married. We never knew it till about ten days ago she spoke of it, and is so forward with child she can go on with her work till Michaelmas, that if my brother can happen of one she go away at midsummer. But at this time a year there is none to be had that are good for anything. If we can but get one that can milk the cow and make the cheese we must make shift and try to live without victuals this quarter, for we shall never get one that can cook. I am sure she

118. The riddle is written on the reverse side of Elizabeth Postlethwaite's letter to Barbara Kerrich Ms 589, f. 62, 26 Feb. 1747.

119. See below Appendix 2, pp. 125-126.

120. *Ibid*, p.126.

was a good servant, but it was a monstrous thing of her not to speak of it sooner. I have write you such a pack of stuff, I don't know where to write my name.

From Elizabeth Postlethwaite
Denton, August 1747

Dear Sister,

Goody Shimon came the day after she came home and stayed all day with me. She tell me you are all well, which is always a pleasure to me, but am sorry to hear you say the hot weather made you so much out of order and so faint. I think you should take all the strengthening things you can contrive.

Mrs Blyford came to see me last week, and she told me there was a journeyman comber came in the coach with Mrs Farrow from Norwich when she came last, and she said by their behaviour, she fancied he courted her. It will be a very sorry match. Mrs Dalling did not intend to go to Norwich till it was more healthful, but if her daughter should be so simple to marry this man I suppose she will not go to live with her at all. Mrs Farrow have brought her little girl with her now and her maid to stay till Michaelmas.

I have taken your advice and wrote to my cousin Johnson not to come till the city be healthful. I believe my brother will be with you next week but am not certain, for he is very much taken up with the painter. He will tell you when he comes what he is doing. Pray tell the Dr I took care Mr Kerrich and Mr Baldry their letters.

From Elizabeth Postlethwaite
Denton, 9 October 1747

Dear Sister,

My brother came from Dersingham very well pleased and said he had spent a week as agreeably as ever he did in his life. He got home of the Tuesday, time enough for my dinner, that I had a feast of them fine fish you were so good to send me; I never tasted nor see any of them before. The figs were my second course that I had a high entertainment and thought they were the best that I ever ate; I was wishing my brother might bring some.

Tell Tilly I thank her for the shells. I'll take great care of her dish clout, and I want to have her here using of it. It is the strangest thing I ever see, it look like the husks of old peas when they are boiled I think. I thought you would be pleased with my brother's present of my dear father's picture. I wish it had been as like as that I have. The painter drew four, and I believe, if he had drawn four more, he couldn't have hit the likeness again.[121]

I am obliged to you for always so kindly remembering me on my birthday. You think I am not so well as I was last year, because I have not been so often in the garden. The reason I have not, is that I find myself tenderer and have catched several colds by going out. Daniel told me before he went away the Dr desired some roots of scarlet lychnis[122] and of sorel[123] by Mr Brock, I'll take care and send them. We had Mr and Mrs Stillingfleet and Mr Barry and Miss Biddy at dinner here on Wednesday. They asked after you and desired their service. I thank you for the receipt.

From Barbara Kerrich
Dersingham, 22 October 1747

Dear Sister,

I wrote in such haste last time, I hadn't time to tell you that I am glad the fish and figs travelled so well that you could get so good a meal of them. I have not tried tar water yet, I am very slow in concluding to take anything of physic.

Sarah desires me to give her duty to you and a thousand thanks for the favour your a being so willing to comply with her request, and wish it may ever lie in her way to be of any service to you. I gave as I told you I would in my last to the nurse and midwife, for you and myself too, for to tell you the truth, the christening is over. I didn't much doubt you would be so good to do it, and she was willing to part with her nurse as soon as she could, as she have been quite well a good while. She never had such a good time nor getting up before, so that I dare say you will excuse our not staying for your answer. I said we had just as much manners as Tom at Bury had when he digged a hole in the garden for his rabbits and then asked my master if he might.

121. *Ibid*, p.126.

122. Lychnis chalcedonica or Jerusalem Cross was commonly used in knots and borders: E. Banks, op. cit., p. 212.

123. Sorel was popular as a salad and thirst quencher.

Mr Phillips was godfather, Mrs Boggas stood for you. I lent Sarah the parlour, for her kitchen is too cold to sit in, so we kept ourselves purely warm and she made us a very pretty dinner and supper. Tilly chose the child's name, she said it should be Detts because her aunt's was so, and it shall be called Miss Detts. Tilly love to talk about the child, but she never trouble herself to nurse it as I thought she would.

The Dr have had three fits of a tertian ague and expected another fit last Saturday evening, but took a vomit about two hours before the expected time, which prevented it, and he have taken the bark 3 or 4 times everyday since that he have had no more of it and he look very well; but it being such a bad time of the year for it, will make us fearful it should return. He thank you for the roots you were so kind to think of for him.

I am surprised at Mrs Baron, though I thought when I saw Mrs Berney and she at Bramerton they seemed to be more pleased with eating and drinking than with anything in the world. Poor Mr Houghton wrote the Dr word he intended to break up housekeeping, but didn't say how he designed to dispose of his poor little family. I think he determined very wisely, for to be sure, he would have been imposed upon by servants. I had a very good letter from my cousin Johnson yesterday with some things she got done for me. She says she is bravely well, but I find the city is sickly still. I don't forget that I owe you for the top of the frock still.

From Elizabeth Postlethwaite
Denton, 12 November 1747?

Dear Sister,

I should have been glad if I could have heard that the Dr had had no return of his ague, and was in hopes the bark would have prevented it, but as it is so slight, I shall hope to have the satisfaction soon of knowing he have lost it though this is a bad time a year for an ague. Pray give him my thanks for thinking of Sir Philip Sidney's *Arcadia* [124] for me, I remember it pleased me very much when I read it before. I will ask Mr Kerrich for it next time I see him.

I think I told you Mrs Dalling was to board with the people that came into the house at Michaelmas. She is very easy with her new way

---

124. *The Arcadia*, a prose romance by Sir Philip Sidney, was published in 1590: Harvey, pp. 36, 754

of life, having no care nor trouble to take about anything, that I believe she think herself quite happy and she have a letter from her daughter every fortnight. And if she don't play the fool and marry that comber, Mrs Dalling will have nothing to give her uneasiness. I haven't heard anything about it since she went from Denton. My brother don't like his new maids. Hannah, which is the upper one I dare say, will be a very careful honest servant. I have a letter to write to my cousin Johnson and it's late that I must conclude.

From Elizabeth Postlethwaite
Denton, 12 December 1747

Dear Sister,

I am glad the Dr have had nothing of his ague and as he escape it, in the cold dismal weather we had the beginning of last week, I hope he will have no more of it.

Your account of the barbecued pig didn't make me sick, but I am glad I wasn't at the entertainment to eat any of it. I should have been sick enough if I had, it must be sad stuff, they had need have strong stomachs that eat, and there was enough of it to feast the mayor and all the town of Lynn.[125] I think they must have a dish made on purpose to hold it, a common one would never do.

I suppose you have got the *Ladies Almanac* by this time and have guessed the riddles, I know you are good at it. My brother think he have found out most of them: the 1st he take to be laughter: the 2d silk worms; the 3d a barber: the 4th a thimble: the 5th garters: the 6th a bell: the 7th a clock: the 8th ink. You must let us know the rest and whether these be right.

The people that live in George Bridges's house, let I told you, I thought was in danger of having the smallpox, I hope will not have it. It's above a month now since the person was there that had it. When Christmas be come and gone which will be soon be now, I shall then begin to think the time is drawing near for your coming, which I wish for with impatience; it is a long time since I see you, I have not coughed since. I hope you will come as soon as you can in the Spring, change of air will be good for the Dr after his illness. My brother did design writing to the Dr but something prevented it.

---

125. Perhaps the feast was celebrating Admiral Hawke's victory over the French at the second Battle of Cape Finisterre 14 Oct. 1747.

From Barbara Kerrich
Dersingham, 27 December 1747?

Dear Sister,

I am very sorry that you have had a return of your cough, I hope it won't continue long and shall be glad to hear that it does not. I desired the Dr to write for me last Monday to let you know the reason you hadn't heard from me so long, for with so much sickness in the family I haven't had a minute's time to spare from Tilly, and I thought you would wonder what was the matter.

As to Molly, I did expect her this Christmas time, but she heard I was angry with her for speaking of my scolding at her at Denton about her husband's coming there. I was a little mad when I first heard she pretended to resent it, because to be sure it was quite improper for him to come there. She sent the child a pretty raree show in a box[126] t'other day and some nice sugar cakes. I suppose I shall see her soon, she is at her sister's at Lynn.

Tilly is mightily pleased with the basket you sent her. You couldn't have sent anything she wanted more, for Johnny, and she go to some market or other every night. The egg they crammed into the basket some way or other, till they have broke it already. If Johnny break anything of hers she is only afraid I should be angry with him, and takes hold of his hand and says, 'Don't cry Johnny, Robin Cock shall mend it,' a carpenter that come here sometimes.

We have borrowed a very entertaining book, but I can't say I have had time either to hear or read much of it, but the Dr is much pleased with it, and it is very much cried up for a clever thing, *The Adventures of David Simple in Search of a Real Friend*.[127] I would have made you a present of it by Mr Brock now, but couldn't get it time enough, but will, against he come next. I fancy it will divert you.

126. A portable show or display. An example c. 1775, shows an artist seated at his easel. 'The picture in progress, seen through a cut-out can be varied by inserting larger pictures at the back of the box': F. Gordon Roe, *The Georgian Child* (1961), p. 21 and note.

127. Sarah Fielding (1710-1768) was the author. It was published in 1744: Harvey, p. 299.

From Barbara Kerrich
Dersingham, 3 February 1748

Dear Sister,

The newsman is not come yet (but I am going to give you an account of the fine bride at Lynn), so if he bring me a letter from you I must answer that last.

I suppose you saw in the papers that Mr Folkes[128] was married to Dr Browne's daughter of Lynn, their finery have been the subject of all the tea tables hereabouts, and it is so remarkable I must give you some account of it. She was married in a white satin sack,[129] the apron[130] part flounced with silver, fine mecklin laced fly cap[131] and hood and tippet[132] and ruffles the same, a pink coloured satin fly petticoat with a deep silver fringe at the bottom, and a broad open lace above it. The Sunday after she was dressed in a suit of clothes, the ground a white corded tabby[133] with very high raised leaves, and flowers of greens and purples the stalks all silver, done all in various ways, a point head, ruffles, tippet and tucker,[134] a blue satin fly petticoat,[135] every seam laced with an open silver lace. Now for her diamonds: on one side of her head she had an 'exsurgent' or 'ensurgent',[136] I don't know the right name. However 'tis feathers of diamonds and a diamond star, on the other side the seven stars in diamonds, before upon her stays: a diamond necklace of small diamonds set like true lovers knots all round the neck, and a solitaire, a diamond girdle, buckles and shoe buckles, a fine repeating watch with his picture set round with diamonds.

The sack she received her company in was scarlet damask, the

128. William Folkes (fl. 1717-1773) of Gray's Inn, 1717, and the Middle Temple, 1720; later Registrar of the Alienation Office. His marriage to Mary, only daughter of Dr Browne, was his second marriage. Like his father-in-law he was a freeman of King's Lynn: Venn, II, p. 156; Hartshorne, p. 133.

129. A kind of lady's loose gown.

130. A garment worn in front of the body to protect clothes.

131. A dress cap of lace gauze, wired into the shape of a butterfly's wings and often edged with jewels.

132. 'A short cape or shoulder covering': A. Buck, op. cit., p. 227.

133. 'A fabric in plain weave, frequently used for silk in this weave': ibid, p. 227.

134. 'The frilled band of linen, muslin or lace edging the neck opening of a gown': ibid, p. 227.

135. A braided (?) petticoat.

136. Exsurgent, 'standing or rising up' suggests the diamonds were mounted to create a tiara-like effect.

The Wedding of Stephen Beckingham and Mary Cox (1729)
Oil painting by William Hogarth
By courtesy of the Metropolitan Museum of Art, Marquand Fund, 1936 (36.111)
All rights reserved The Metropolitan Museum of Art, New York

apron part flounced with silver, and robings[137] all silver, the side seams of the sack laid all the way down with two open broad silver laces of a side, a fine laced fly cap flowered gauze ruffles and tippet, with silver lace mixed with snail or something upon it. As to the bridegroom, I don't understand his dress so well, but it was cut velvets,[138] fine waistcoats etc. The newsman is now come, but have brought no letter from you. I hope it is not illness prevented your writing. Pray be so kind to send this letter to my mother. I have given her an account of the bride too.

From Barbara Kerrich
Dersingham, 2 March 1748

Dear Sister,

I drank tar water about a week, I like it mighty well, it was very agreeable to my stomach, but my bowels have never been right since that disorder in them. I have had something like it several times and sickness in my stomach, that I have been forced to take tincture of rhubarb[139] twice or thrice o'week, but when my bowels are more settled I shall try it again.

The Dr had forgot that writing, but he had an imperfect notion of some agreement, but how or when, he had quite forgot, and Mr Baldry gave no reason why he sent so much short, he might have said according to agreement. We heard the Bishop was to be married to Lady Compton,[140] the Dr says if that be the name it must be the Earl of Northampton's sister.

Tilly begin to spell very prettily for the time she have learnt: I hardly know how she learnt her letters, for I never set about teaching her in earnest till this Winter, and then only when she liked it, that now she make it quite a diversion and can read almost any little word without stopping at it. Mrs Hoste gave her the prettiest book for a child to learn by that ever I saw, there's spelling and fables and stories

137. 'Revers extending from the neck down the bodice opening of a gown': A. Buck, op. cit., p. 227.

138. Patterned velvets.

139. To combat 'weakness of the stomach, indigestion, laxity of the intestines, fluxes, cholicky and such complaints': Buchan, p. 698.

140. Mary, daughter of Hatton Compton grandson of the 2nd Earl of Northampton was the Bishop's third wife. She was about 40 at the time of marriage and died in 1780: G.E.C., V, pp. 91-92.

which she is very fond of, and she will always know what she is reading of, and love it very much. She is a little displeased at me for not wording her letter as she liked, for I made her spell every word as I guided her hand, and when we had done, she said, 'What occasion had you to say I hadn't time to use Jack so bad, couldn't you have said I am better to him? As for the time, why I have time enough to knock him all to pieces if I had a mind.' She have wrote some of the direction herself alone. You would be surprised how she will attend when I am reading any play or story, and how earnest to know how it end.

There is lately come out *The History of Miss Clarissa Harlowe* by the editor of *Pamela* and 'tis thought the same author.[141] We have borrowed it and the Dr thinks it a very good thing so far as he have seen of it, but there's only two volumes published yet, and we are left wholly in the dark as to the catastrophe. Miss Clarissa is a most amiable character, but we leave her in so perplexing circumstances that I think long for the other volumes. Here is a great many more persons than in *Pamela*. When the other volumes come out I will contrive you a sight of them, if we shouldn't buy them, but I suppose we shall, I dare say they would please you.

We are in a great hurry here about cambrics, for it seems the act is to be very strict and I see in the papers they are going to make another to explain and enforce that.[142] It will make a vast deal of trouble as well as charge. I have neither ruffles nor head things but what are cambric, nor Tilly, nor I suppose nobody else, 'tis so good and strong I can't think what we shall wear, we must go to clapping of muslins and they are as rotten as muck. I shall be very thankful for the present you intend me by Mr Brock, you couldn't send me anything I want more, I have none but what I buy, and Ruth and Sukey are great strys(?). The Dr a little wonder that my brother have not given him his thoughts of the epitaph.

141. The first two volumes of Samuel Richardson's *Clarissa Harlowe* were published in 1747, the complete five-volume edition in 1748: Harvey, pp. 173, 694.

142. An Act 'for prohibiting the wearing and importation of Cambrics and French lawns, 18 Geo II, cap. 36 (1744-1745)' was followed by another 'Act for explaining, amending and enforcing an Act made in the 18th year of the reign of His Present Majesty. .21 Geo. II, cap. 26 (1747-1748)'.

From Elizabeth Postlethwaite
Denton, 10 March 1748

Dear Sister,

I am very glad you like tar water and that it do agree with you so well, and should have thought it would have done you good for that disorder in your bowels as it's reckoned good for fevers.

My brother went to London last week, I had a letter from him on Monday and he hope he shall be at home again this week. He talked of writing to the Dr before he went, that sure he will when he return, and give him an account what he intend to do about that money. He have not paid me a farthing yet, nor I him for my board, but there will be a year due to him at a Lady, then perhaps he will reckon with me for that and pay me the other money too. But I don't know rightly what is coming to me. I think I have only one half year's interest paid me yet.

Tilly is very good to learn her book so prettily and your way of teaching is certainly the best way to make her love and take delight in it, and her being so fond of stories will make her eager of learning, that I dare say she will soon be a good reader. I should be pleased to hear her so desirous of knowing what she read, it is very pretty of her and very extraordinary at her years. I should have laughed to have heard her talk about Jack. Pray tell her I'll write to her soon. I hope her uncle will ask her to come this year, I am sure I shall be very much concerned and disappointed if he don't, for I have set my heart upon seeing you. Those tin things you speak of have been gone a long time, I have some notion we gave them to some little girl, but I have forgot who. *The History of Miss Clarissa Harlowe* my brother intend buying now he is at London. I shall be in haste to read it, you give so good a character of it. I shouldn't have concluded my letter yet, but Mrs Hervey is come to make me a visit so can write no further. This letter is from Mr Baldry.

From Barbara Kerrich
Dersingham, 26 March 1748

Dear Sister,

I am not willing to miss any opportunity that I have of writing to you, knowing you are always glad to hear that we are all well, only I have got a little cold in one of my eyes which is a little inflamed that I can't write much, it water so.

You will be sorry as well as I when you know that Mr Phillips who brings this, brings the sad news of poor Sarah's death, to her father and mother. She died last night about ten o'clock. She had a violent fever both before and after her miscarriage, and 'tis feared took too many opiates of her own head, because poor creature, she could take no rest. I am very much concerned for her and shall want her for a thousand things, and to see so many motherless babes almost break my heart, though she have so many friends they are all like to be well taken care on. Little Martin is to come to one of his uncles at Ditchingham to learn to be a brickmaker, and her father they think will take Billy, and we shall take Johnny and Mr Phillips take Jemmy and Betsy, and her sister Nanny have taken Tommy. I shall be glad to hear by the carrier on Wednesday that you are pretty well.

From Elizabeth Postlethwaite
Denton, 31 March 1748

Dear Sister,

I was very much surprised to hear of poor Sarah's death, I am really concerned for her. It's a good thing the children are so well taken care of, I am glad of it. You're very kind to take Johnny. You will want the poor creature, she was useful to you upon many accounts, I have often heard you say. Tilly I suppose is vexed for her.

My brother was not at home that morning Mr Phillips called here, I wished he had. I just spoke to him out at a window, but I dare not stand long for fear of catching cold. He seem a civil well behaved man, I was pleased with him. I have been a good deal out of order for sometime with something of a colicky disorder and a very great uneasiness in my stomach, but not inclined to cough. I am glad to hear that you are all well and hope the little cold you have will soon go off. Mrs Hoste's behaviour was indeed very respectful and handsome.

You quite mistake me about Clarissa if you think I would have had her have had Lovelace after so vile an action: no, it was impossible indeed so fine a character as she could think of such a wicked wretch as he for a husband, for to be sure, only the very sight of him after such a horrid deed must be most hateful to her. What I meant was, I would not have had him drawn so black a character that she might have had the glory and pleasure to have reclaimed him and been happy with him, but after he had run such lengths in wickedness it could not end otherwise nor better than it did, that's certain. Belford I like, he and Miss Howe are poor Clarissa's chief friends.

Johnny Baldry was at Benacre on Monday to carry my mother her money, and by the account he give of her health, I am afraid she shouldn't continue long. I am a going to lay on a blister to remove the uneasiness in my stomach.

From Elizabeth Postlethwaite
Denton, 16 June 1748

Dear Sister,

I am very glad to hear you got home so well and that Tilly held out so well, I think she is a very good traveller for so young one. Mr Kerrich tell me the Dr catched cold in his journey, I hope it's not a bad one as you said nothing about it. I am glad the smallpox is ceased for the Dr's sake, but I did not expect to hear it would, for indeed I thought of having you here again so that we should at least have spent the Summer together which would have pleased me very much.

I give you thanks for the nun's hood, it is purely warm, I think I shall be in no danger of catching cold in my head when I have that on, and I thank you for the lily of the valley roots.[143] I had Will set them under the currant bushes of the right hand, as you go down the steps out of the courtyard. The pennyroyal water[144] I like very well, it agree with me, I tried it this week and I will try to still some as soon as I can get the pennyroyal. The candied ginger will do you good and I dare say it wouldn't me, for it would have heart burnt me that I would not have taking any from you.

I sent my mother your letter and am pleased with what you have said and thank you for it, I think it can't possibly be taken amiss. I am a going to write to my cousin Johnson to come, you have sent her a great many things. She will be pleased with them and go hard to work as soon as she come. She make any old thing look tight and whole, she never lose anything for want of mending, that every bit of rag is well bestowed upon her. I am very sorry for the news of Mrs Gregson for their own sakes as well as yours, for I think you will lose a good neighbour of them. I have sent the receipt for the tansy.

143. Lily of the Valley, Convallaria majalus, widely grown in borders and knots: E. Banks, op. cit., p. 210.

144. Penny Royal, Mentha-Pulegium, a traditional herbal remedy was recommended as a cure for venomous bites and spots, ulcers, mouth sores, bruises and as a purgative. It was reputedly effective in expelling a dead child from the womb together with the afterbirth. Buchan merely notes its use in mixtures and juleps to hysteric patients: Culpeper, op. cit., pp. 266-267; Buchan, p. 703.

From Barbara Kerrich
Dersingham, 19 July 1748

Dear Sister,

Ever since I wrote to you last I have been very poorly, so faint o' mornings I am forced to rest 2 or 3 times before I can get my things on. I drink chocolate every morning and have been blooded, for I find my ailment is breeding. I suppose I am ten weeks gone, for I have known nothing to the contrary since I came home.

I wonder I haven't miscarried yet, this put me upon great difficulties as to servants, for if I should not miscarry I may want three, but if I should (which is most likely), I shall have no patience with keeping three any longer, and I like the character of that servant you sent me word of, but I think she ask too great wages. I did make a resolution never to give above 3 pound a year again.[145] If I do give her anything more it must be only upon condition that she does my work thoroughly well when then she knows it, nor she must not scruple bringing coals upstairs in a morning for the fire, for when I have but two, the upper maid must do that, which I would have her know. Because servants make a great rout[146] about fetching coals or wood, I like they should know the worst of their work as well as the best. I dare say I shall like her by your account of her, but put off making a bargain with her as long as you can, because I suppose I shall soon send you word that I have miscarried, and then to be sure I will have her.

You say your pennyroyal water does not taste well. I have heard Mrs Hoste say it taste of the fire at first. Therefore she let it stand 3 or 4 days or a week before she put a cork in, only a bit of paper laid upon the top of the bottle till that taste fly off. I think you managed nicely not to melt the bottom of the still, for Mrs Captain Hoste was telling me she only forgot to put sand between the bottom and the frame and she melted a hole in hers.

I must think it was very kind of the Bishop and respectful too, to call upon you at Denton. I am pleased with him for it and I think you entertained him very prettily. I thank God Tilly is got finely well again and desires her duty. Mr Rand[147] and Dr Pyle dined with us t'other day and invited us very much to go to both their houses upon a frolic.

145. In eighteenth century London general servants were paid between £3 and £5 a year: A. Laurence op. cit., p. 136.

146. 'A squabble, a noise': Bailey.

147. Brock Rand (1697-1753), Antiquary. Rector of Leverington, Cambridgeshire 1724-1753 and of Newton, Isle of Ely 1731-1753: Venn, III, p. 418.

I am not well enough at present. Poor Mary Brady that was, is very ill of a violent fever and have been this fortnight. Sukey go to see her every night; she came home full of tears last night, she was very bad.

From Elizabeth Postlethwaite
Denton, 29 July 1748

Dear Sister,

I am glad your complaint is nothing more than breeding and hope I shall be able to give you joy of the increase of your family, for I beg you would be very careful of yourself and prevent if possible miscarrying, you know it is a very great injury, and weakening to your constitution. I think you took Mrs Townshend's drink when you were with child of Tilly and hope you will now; pray omit nothing that is likely to be of service to you.[148]

I am vexed to tell you I am disappointed of Mrs Howman's maid for you. She have a mother alive who will not let her go so far from her, the maid was vexed at it for she was very willing to come. I had one came this week that I believe will do if you should want her. She live now with Mrs Arrowsmith, she liked her so well that she would not have parted with her, but that she is to have a servant that lived with her a great many years come to her again at Michaelmas, that was always a very great favourite. This maid make no scruple about doing any of your work but seem as if she could do it with ease; she is a good, clever, clean looking servant. Mrs Rackham sent her daughter with her and she tell me Mrs Arrowsmith think she do not iron linen quite as neat as some servants, but can do it very well. I told her I couldn't hire her till I had an answer from you. She desired she might know as soon as she could.

I was highly pleased with the Bishop's visit, I thought it very good and kind in him to take so much notice of us. I didn't I believe tell you that Mr and Mrs Fairman came to dinner here that day to meet his Lordship, and Dr Fowle came in the afternoon. They were all unexpected visitors. My cousin Johnson is here and send her respects and thanks for the things you sent her and her daughter. I must once more before I conclude, beg of you to be particularly careful of yourself. It will concern me very much to hear you have miscarried.

148. See above, p. 39.

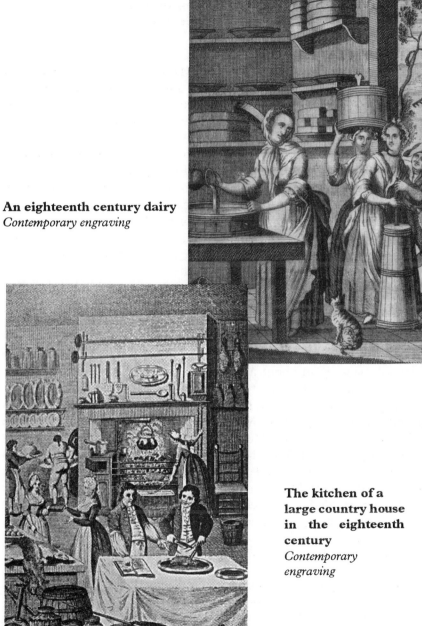

An eighteenth century dairy
Contemporary engraving

The kitchen of a large country house in the eighteenth century
Contemporary engraving

From Elizabeth Postlethwaite
Denton, 12 August 1748

Dear Sister,

I am sorry you complain so much of faintness, I wish I may hear in your next letter you get better, but am glad you are in no danger at present of miscarrying, and by care I hope you will not.

I have no luck at all with maids for you. I can't have Mrs Arrow-smith's, her friends won't let her go so far from them. I have been disappointed of four, I have inquired again but at present don't hear of any that will do, but if I should hear of one that is likely to fit you I will write again next week. If you can hear of any about you I think you had better not depend upon me because I have such bad success, and Michaelmas will soon be here. My brother have hired only an upper maid, yet he have not heard of a cook that is fit for him. Nan go to be cook at Mrs Smith's of Topcroft, Hannah have got a place at Bungay.

My cousin Johnson is here still, my brother is very kind and civil to her. She told him you desired her to take the still home with her, but he talk now of getting it made fit for his own use and is unwilling to part from it, that if he won't let you have it I'll take care and still pennyroyal water for you what you want. They tell me that the penny royal will be as good about Michaelmas time as it was in the Spring, that if the still be fit I design to still some for you and myself.

Mr Jacky Gooch[149] went to Benacre about a fortnight ago and was so obliging as to call here. My brother was just walked out, but he came up and spoke to me. He seem very free and good natured, I was mightily pleased with him, he is all life and spirit. Justice Kerrich's lady[150] was brought to bed last Wednesday of a son. I told Goodman Brady his daughter Mary had a great desire to see him. He say he should be very glad to see her and is concerned she is so ill, but he is quite unable to go so long a journey, he grow old and infirm, he can't go through with a day's work now, but desire to be kindly remembered to all his daughters.

---

149. John Gooch D.D. (1730-1804), son of Thomas Gooch, Bishop of Norwich and Hannah, daughter of Sir John Miller 4th Baronet of Lavant, his second wife; Prebend of Ely 1753-1804. A portrait of John Gooch (1777) by Thomas Kerrich was included in the Benacre Sale, 9, 10, 11, May 2000 (lot 192): Venn, II, p. 232; introduction, note 17 above.

150. Simon Kerrich's third wife was Ann the eldest daughter of Thomas Manning of Starston Gent: NRO MC 1578/1.

From Barbara Kerrich
Dersingham, 22 August 1748

Dear Sister,

I am sorry I have given you so much trouble about maids, and I don't know whether one that is so wholly a stranger would have liked me, or I them. I have heard of one but have not seen her yet, she live with a clergyman at Rising.[151] I shall do the better as Fanny is to stay with me all Winter or till I am brought to bed, so that she will learn her how to do all her business, for Fanny don't intend to go to service any more, but in the Spring bind herself to a mantua-maker at Bury, she have an aunt live near there. Ruth is to go to be cook at a gentleman's at Lynn and is to have three pound a year. She would have her mother know it when you see her, for fear she should get her a place as little Martin wrote to desire she would, but Ruth never heard from them since. She is highly pleased with the thoughts of living at Lynn, one of Mr Phillips's daughters is upper maid at the same place.

If my brother like to keep the still I shall be thankful to you for some pennyroyal water, for I have but very little. Don't you find yours mend with keeping? But to be sure it couldn't be done with so regular a heat as if you had the frame of the still to set it upon. I am very poorly, I don't know for these two months that I have been two hours tolerably well, but every forenoon I am right down ill, I never was so constantly ill when I was with child before. I had a fit of an ague last Thursday but had no more since. I haven't been like miscarrying yet, which I wonder at.

There is a great deal of company at Mr Gregson's: Miss Branthwayt and her brother and Mr and Mrs Bates, and young Mr Gregson. They have been there this week in order to take leave of Dersingham, and last night they concluded that Mr and Mrs Gregson are to stay at Dersingham, and Mr and Mrs Bates are to come and board with them. So how matters are I don't know, but I like they should stay better than strangers to come for they are good neighbours in the main. It was prettily done of young Mr Gooch to call upon you, I have wrote till I am quite faint. I should be glad if you could send me one or both my gallipots[152] by Mr Brock.

151. Castle Rising.
152. A small earthenware glazed pot, used for ointments etc.

From Elizabeth Postlethwaite
Denton, 2 September 1748

Dear Sister,

It concern me very much that you continue so low and poorly. I am afraid you have not made that drink of Mrs Townshend's, I wonder you should not, I think it's quite necessary for you. I am sure you want strengthening things and though you do not at present fear miscarrying, you may perhaps without taking this drink, as you are so weak. I am sorry you have had a fit of an ague, I hope you will have no more of it. I am glad Mrs Fanny is to stay with you till you are brought to bed, for a new servant without her would have been a great deal of trouble for you, now that you are so much out of order. I have sent Goody Shimon word her daughter Ruth have got a place.

We have had the favour of a visit from Mr Gooch of Benacre, he went to Harleston Fair[153] to buy sheep on Monday and came here Tuesday in the forenoon, stayed till Wednesday morning. I thought it very obliging in him, I was pleased very much with his visit. He did purpose being here of the Monday night too, but was hindered. Mr Jacky Gooch called here again in his return to Cambridge and brought us a couple of fine melons from Benacre. I sent your letter to my mother by Mr Gooch.

My pennyroyal water do taste better than it did. If I can get the still made fit for use you shan't want pennyroyal water, but I am afraid our blacksmith can't do it. He don't seem to have a right notion of it. I bid him go to some apothecaries and look at their stills to see if he could make out how it should be done, I have a great desire to have it fit to use.

My brother have given me the two first volumes of *Clarissa*. I don't see in the newspapers that the two last are come out yet. I have but one gallipot of yours, the little one that you sent the currant jelly in when you sent the venison. I'll take care and send it by Mr Brock. My cousin Johnson is gone home, I am going to write to her.

153. The second annual fair began 29th August, the Feast of the Beheading of John the Baptist and was an eight-day event. There was also a midsummer fair on 24th June, St John the Baptist's Nativity: Blomefield, V, p. 356.

From Elizabeth Postlethwaite
Denton, 20 September 1748

Dear Sister,

I am sorry you hold so poorly, but if I had had no letter I should have thought you had been worse or miscarried that it would have made me very uneasy. I am glad you have not and that you have made the drink which I hope will prevent it and make you stronger. I am glad Mrs Hoste have given you some pennyroyal water, for I don't know whither I shall get any for you. I have sent you a taste of mine, it's all I have. I didn't still above 3 quarters of a pint but 'tisn't so good as yours, so there's enough of it.

I had heard the Bishop's lady was breeding, I suppose the same person that told you it might also tell you that the vacant prebendary of Ely was designed for Mr Nicholls, and if he accept it he is to resign Redenhall, and the talk is here that that is to be disposed of to one of Sir Charles Castleton's sons[154] who is to have Miss Fereman, the truth of this I don't know, but I am sure the Bishop will use his interest and get it for him if he can. Mrs Fereman[155] don't approve of the match for her daughter for he have no estate, only a small living, and she told his Lordship when he was here that he must get him one. I was amazed to hear her talk in so free a manner, but she is a great favourite.

You are so kind never to forget my birthday, I am obliged to you for it. I had Mrs Blyford here, she told me she would come and drink my health in the fine wine I had made that I told you was to be sack, but 'tis not sack nor anything else that's good for it's sad stuff, it's more like physic than anything. If it had been good, you should have had a bottle of it by Mr Brock.

Justice Kerrich have buried his youngest little girl, she died of a fever. Mr Brock told me he heard by Mr Simpson that the Dr was either gone or going to London. Poor Goodman Brady want to know

154. Sir Charles Castleton's two younger sons were clergymen, John (1697-1777), 8th Baronet, Vicar of Gorleston, Suffolk, 1722-1777, was the favourite candidate for the living according to Elizabeth. Miss Fereman was his prospective wife. The youngest son, Edward (1708-1794), 11th Baronet, eventually became Rector of Thornham and Holme, 1761-1794. Her sister thought Edward the likelier of the two, but in the event the living was granted to Henry Stebbing D.D. (1687-1763): G.E.C., II, p. 128: Ms 589 f. 69, Elizabeth Postlethwaite to Barbara Kerrich 7 Oct. 1747 and f.92, 21 Oct. 1748; Venn, IV p. 153.

155. Possibly the wife of James Ferman of Christ's College, Cambridge, 1715: Venn, II, p. 132.

how Mary do and the rest of his children. I suppose he would be glad if they would write him such a fine letter and send by Mr Brock, as he had from them last year. I think you have my mother's receipt for grape wine, if it be not too much trouble for to search it out, I should be glad to have it by Mr Brock.

From Barbara Kerrich
Dersingham, 22 September 1748

Dear Sister,

I give you thanks for your pennyroyal water, I dare not taste of it now, but I think it smell very well.

The same person that told us about the Bishop's lady did say that he heard Mr Nicholls was to have the prebendary and Mr Castleton to have Redenhall. We thought it had been Sir Charles Castleton's son who has a small living near here, but he is married to a clergyman's daughter in this part of the country, so it can't be him, how many sons have Sir Charles Castleton[156] clergymen? The Bishop do barter and bargain away things strangely. Sure, he might have happened of a living for him now he have always something falling to dispose of. Sure, he'll give my brother Kerrich something if he take away his curacy, for I suppose this man will reside.

It's a pity your sack proved so bad, but I think nothing can taste pleasant that have rue in it. It was Charles and Mr Simpson's first proposal of the Dr's going to St Albans about some business to Mr Raye and from thence to London. They are always full of schemes, but the Dr couldn't conveniently go then, and now he has laid aside the thoughts of it.

I am quite weary and sick that you must excuse the shortness of my letter. Tilly have a mind to write to you when I have rested myself a little, so she'll send her duty herself, if we have time. I have sent the silk at last, pray give it my brother Kerrich.

156. Sir Charles Castleton (1659-1745), 6th Baronet, Rector of Gillingham 1692-1745: G.E.C. II, p.127.

From Elizabeth Postlethwaite
Denton, 30 October 1748

Dear Sister,

You will wonder you have not heard from me, I wrote last week and Payn never called for it. I am vexed at the disappointment, I am afraid you will think I am ill or very careless to be so long without writing.

I give you thanks for the pineapple, it came safe, and very sound it was. I like it mighty well, the flavour is very different from any fruit I ever tasted. I could eat but a little bit at a time, I sent for Mrs Blyford before I cut it, I had a mind she should see it whole. She admire it very much, she never tasted so fine a fruit in her life. She was pleased that you desired she should taste of it. I sent Mrs Bream a slice which the old lady was pleased with, they both send their service.

Mrs Stillingfleet have been to see me, she dined here but he couldn't. He was obliged to dine at Alburgh at a fine christening he had there, but came in the afternoon. They desire their service and asked after you, and drank your healths. She is very brisk and full of spirits. Poor Mr Dalling I doubt is quite ruined, though I suppose my mother might send you word of it as she did me, of his going to the Bishop to borrow 30 pound. It was a most strange thought to go there, he must be in the utmost straits difficulties imaginable, I am really much concerned for him. He was a little while ago sued for forty shillings by the man that keep the King's Head in this town.

The addition I did intend writing into my will myself, but the design of sending it to Mr Sayer was that I might know his opinion of whether it would do without the surrender, but if he think the surrender necessary I must run the hazard of my brother's doing cross things by me. I have not seen Mr Kerrich since he carried it to Mr Sayer, and if it must be done the sooner the better, for life is uncertain.

My cousin Johnson is here and we all drank Tilly's health on her birthday, wishing her a great many happy years. She is a very good girl for learning her book so prettily, I think she come on apace, she hardly knew her letters when she was here. I believe she will soon be able to read my letter if she go on so fast. My brother is gone to Benacre.

From Elizabeth Postlethwaite
Denton, 10 December 1748

Dear Sister,

I begin to write today, but won't finish my letter till tomorrow because I expect one from you then.

You said in your last letter you couldn't think what Justice Kerrich would do with all his money, he is soon taken from it poor man. He was at chapel on Sunday in the forenoon and taken ill there and died about twelve o'clock at night, but to be sure, the Dr will have a better and more particular account from his brother than I can give.

My brother is altering his garden. He have laid the bleaching yard[157] into it as the Dr proposed; you can't imagine the addition it is to the look of the garden. I didn't think it would have been so great an improvement. I shall want very much that the Dr and you should see it when it's finished. I wish it were my house that I could ask you, I am sure you would like it. My brother don't go to London so soon as he designed, it won't be till after Christmas day now, but I had wrote to my cousin Johnson to come and I expect her tonight.

We are a little frightened at some robberies that have been committed hereabouts. One Mrs Lemmon, a widow lady on Monday evening about seven o'clock, as she was sat at supper 5 men got into the house and robbed her of her money and plate and other things to the value of 500 pound. They attempted Lady Ward's[158] house too, but there they were prevented getting in, but a blacksmith at Hedenham they got a 100 pound from. It put us in fears and make us upon our guard.

I hope you intend having a man midwife[159] and shall be glad to hear it's well over with you, I pray God send you a good time. My cousin Johnson came last night and brought your letter. I am sorry Mr Ensley is dead, but hope this gentleman's judgement is as good as his in such cases. I am vexed you seem to fear your strength and courage,

---

157. The bleaching yard, where sheets were hung out to dry was on the eastward side of the Rectory: NRO TER/53/3/10 25 June 1735.

158. Lady Susan Ward, daughter of William Randall of Yarmouth, merchant, widow of Sir Edward Ward, 5th Baronet of Bixley (died 1737): G.E.C., III, p. 139.

159. Male midwives became increasingly fashionable in the early eighteenth century. Matilda Postlethwaite's niece had the services of a man midwife from Yarmouth in 1747: R. Porter, op. cit., p. 30; Ms 588 f. 210, Matilda Postlethwaite to Barbara Kerrich 23 April 1747.

but though you have been so poorly all along, I hope you will want neither when the time come, and as you have had strength to go your full time, God Almighty I hope will support and carry you through. Remember the advice Lady Davers gave Pamela, 'think little and hope much'. I wish I were near enough to have dear little Tilly with me at the time.

I conclude with the usual good wishes of the approaching season, and may the new year make you happy in a son.[160] I have sent two bottles of pennyroyal water, if you want more you shall have it when Mr Brock come again.

From Barbara Kerrich
Dersingham, 18 January 1749

Dear Sister,

The Dr would have wrote to you to be sure last week if I had been brought to bed. I still hold up, and I think I have been better this last week than I have been a great while. I have no reason to think but that the child is alive and well at present, and as to my feet being swelled, they were so with Tilly and the child I had before her, only I am bigger and more cumbersome to myself, and have been all the time so ill that make me more thoughtful about it.

We are continually hearing of robberies hereabouts now, they spread all the country pilfering in the daytime, though we have heard of some houses that have been beset in the night. There was a maid-servant walking t'other day in a lane beyond Snettisham, and she happened of a man and woman who stripped her of all her clothes but her shift, and that they tied about her head.

We have read the 3 last volumes of *Clarissa*, and Tilly said 'tell my aunt how pretty 'tis', and indeed they are reckoned prodigious finely done by everybody that have read them, and all agree there's no reading them without shedding a good many tears, but my husband say 'Stop there, for you'll let your sister into it, that she won't have half the pleasure in reading it.' We have given Sukey the bark, and she have had nothing on it since, which is about a month.

160. Thomas Kerrich, her only son to survive, was born 4 February 1748.

From Elizabeth Postlethwaite
Denton, 23 June 1749

Dear Sister,

I thank God I have had no return of my ague and have pretty well recovered my strength, but must grow stronger yet or I shan't be able to perform a journey to Dersingham this year, which I expect to, for my brother is quite weary of housekeeping; the expense is so great he say he can't afford it and intend going on no longer than Michaelmas,[161] and he know that I write you word of it that make me think he won't alter his mind this time.

When I write again I shall be more certain, and the sooner I come the better, that I may quite recover the disorder and fatigue of my journey before Winter. I am vexed poor little Tommy's humour increase, I think you are right to let Dr Kerrich know it. Mrs Kerrich is now at Harleston with her sister. I shall have an opportunity on Sunday to let Goody Shimon know about Ruth. I design to nurse a little, at least I can rock the cradle: that will be good employ for me, for I hope I shall be able to get to you.

Miss Smith of Harleston and one of Mrs Pepit's daughters, an agreeable young creature far beyond Miss Smith, came to see me and Mrs Smith sent her compliments to you and the Dr, and wish you joy of your son. I have been reading of *Tom Jones,*[162] I suppose you have had it. It's a book very much admired and I dare say you like it if you have read it, I am very much pleased with it .I heartily wish the Dr a good journey. Mr Brock called here, I gave Molly Baldry her fan on Sunday. She send her services to Tilly and many thanks, and is pleased with it.

From Elizabeth Postlethwaite
Denton, 7 July 1749

Dear Sister,

My brother keep his resolution so that I shall at last trouble you and please myself with the thoughts of spending my time very much to

161. 'He (John Postlethwaite) says he can't afford it no longer' i.e. the expense of living at Denton Rectory: Ms 591 f. 206, Barbara Kerrich to Samuel Kerrich 3 July 1749.

162.*Tom Jones, a Foundling* (1749) by Henry Fielding (1704-1754): Harvey, pp. 298-299, 824.

my satisfaction when with you, and hope we shall be quite happy together.

When I was to have come before, you mentioned that room for me where your worked bed is, but there is no chimney and I can't be without a fire in my chamber, but as your best chamber chimney is against that chamber, I should think a fireplace could be easily made without much trouble or expense, that is if you and the Dr approve of it, and think it proper to mention it to Lord Orford's Steward. And if he should think the charge too much, I should not be unwilling to be at half myself for I should like to have that room, and the furniture I have in this will do in that, for my brother tell me he will give me everything that I have in my chamber here.

As to coming I have no thoughts of venturing any way but in a horse litter, I wouldn't pretend to it, I am very sensible I couldn't bear any other way, but I fancy the body of a landau would be better than a coach because it's larger, for it must be contrived so to lay a bed in and room enough for somebody to be with, but I will leave the Dr and you to manage with Slack. I design sending my things before harvest if I can, but I can't set a time yet for my own coming, I have work to do for my brother first.

I must beg the favour of you to let your maid make me some raisin wine. I am glad poor Tommy is easier.[163] Mr Kerrich think vine leaves would be better than oil case, they would not draw so much, and he say perhaps oil case may draw too much. Goody Shimon is quite willing Ruth should live with you.

From Barbara Kerrich
Dersingham, 11 July 1749

Dear Sister,

I wouldn't have you call your coming here a trouble, for I hope it will be a great pleasure and comfort to us both.

The Dr is not come home yet, he sent me word he set out last Saturday morning for St Albans to settle some affairs with Mr Raye who lives there, so I don't know when I am to expect him. I hope I shall have a letter tonight. If the chimney cannot be done this Summer you shall have the best room till it can, for they are very slow in getting anything done for tenants. We will manage everything about the

163. Thomas Kerrich had been inoculated against smallpox: Ms 591 f. 205 30 June 1749.

landau for you, won't you try Mrs Baker's chair that you may be a little used to it by degrees before you come, and engage my brother Kerrich to come with you? I will go about your raisin wine as soon as this washing is over.

Tommy's face is just well, he left off his oil case cap last Sunday sennight that did not draw so much as the vine leaves. He have an issue in his arm which do mighty well, and I hope will do him a great deal of good, he is very brisk.

From Elizabeth Postlethwaite
Denton, 4 August 1749

Dear Sister,

My brother's maid is going to Norwich tomorrow and she shall go to Slack and see how he go on. You tell me I must get two strong carthorses, here is two in this town I can have, but I have seen in brewers carts, horses that seem I think more able to bear such a burthen than any common carthorses, and if you think they would do better I suppose Slack could get a couple. Musn't there be a man to ride upon each horse? If there must, I believe Goodman Brady will be one of my attendants, he have a great mind to see his children. I fancied Wymondham would be the best way because I thought I should meet with most baiting places and I knew it was nearest. My first day's journey must be to Stratton and the next day to Wymondham. I wish the journey over, for Mr Kerrich discourage me very much and make me fuller of fears than otherwise I should be. My cousin Johnson have been ill and is but poorly that I think not have her come with me, for fear I should want more help than she will be able to give me, that I design to take the maid with me. I have promised my bird to Miss Peak, for I think I shall have enough to do to take care of myself, but tell Tilly I shall bring the cage and she may put a bird into that and hang it in my room.

From Barbara Kerrich
Dersingham, 18 October 1749

Dear Sister,

I thank you for inquiring so kindly after poor little Tommy, I thank God his fever have left him, but he have cut no teeth yet. He look poorly and I am afraid won't look better till he have cut some, we have thought one or two have been near cutting a good while.

You say I have said nothing about Tilly a good while, now I shall tell you what a sad little rogue she is for plays. We have some good players come to Snettisham and have been to see *The Beaux Strategem*,[164] and *The Journey to London*. The entertainment after that was *The King and the Miller*, an exceeding good thing, I never saw it before, but Tilly entered into the plot so that she gave her papa a very good account of it, and put me in mind of several things that had escaped me. Tonight she beg to go to *The Recruiting Officer*. She make surprising remarks upon any story or play that she hear, so her papa tell her he will give her this one more.

To tell you the truth I made Mrs Norsa[165] a visit first. My Lord[166] asked me several times very kindly, I believe it was taken well, for she soon returned it. I wouldn't tell you of my visit because I didn't know what you would think of it, for I don't know but it might be cutting a bold stroke. She is a very agreeable woman, and nobody ever behaved better in her station. She have everybody's good word and bear great sway at Houghton. She is everything but a lady. She came here in a landau and six horses, and one Mr Paxton[167] a young clergyman with her. Mrs Masters[168] is now here to stay a week or a fortnight and from hence to Lynn, to try what subscriptions she can get in this part of the country. She desires her compliments to you.

164. George Farquhar (1678-1707) was the author of *The Beaux Strategem* (1707) and *The Recruiting Officer* (1706).*The Journey to London*, usually known as *The Provok'd Wife* was written by Vanbrugh, completed by Cibber and first performed in 1728. Robert Dodsley's *The King and the Miller of Mansfield* was first performed in 1737: Harvey, 74, 292, 669, 685; Brian Allen, *Francis Hayman* (Ex. Catalogue New Haven and London 1987), No. 63.

165. Hannah Norsa, (c.1715-1785) actress, daughter of a Jewish tavern keeper and subsequently Lord Orford's mistress, made her name as Polly in Gay's *The Beggar's Opera* at Covent Garden, Dec. 1732-Jan. 1733: Ernest. L. Avery et al., *The London Stage 1660-1800* (5 Pts. Southern Illinois U.S.A. 1961), 3, pp. cxxxiv, 134, 256; Louise Lippincott, *Selling Art in Georgian London: The Rise of Arthur Pond* (New Haven and London 1983), p. 68.

166. Robert Walpole, 2nd Earl of Orford (1701-1751), eldest son of Sir Robert Walpole and his first wife, Catherine Shorter.

167. William Paxton (fl. 1742-1795) Rector of Taplow, Bucks., 1788: Venn, III, p. 322.

168. Mary Masters (d. 1759?), poet, author of *Familiar Letters And Poems On Several Occasions* (1755). She became acquainted with Barbara Kerrich and her sister, probably thanks to Matilda Postlethwaite: D.N.B. XIII, p. 25.

Miss Hannah Norsa (1794)
Born 1715, died 1785.
Etching by R. Clamp
after Bernard Lens II,
By courtesy of the National
Portrait Gallery, London

Strolling Actresses in a Barn (1738)
Engraving by William Hogarth
By courtesy of the Witt Library, Courtauld Institute, London

From Elizabeth Postlethwaite
Denton, 27 October 1749

Dear Sister,

I am glad Tommy have lost his fever, and I hope to hear in your next letter that he have cut some of his teeth.

You should have called Tilly a pretty little rogue, for I think she so and it is very extraordinary such a child as she should be capable of giving any account of a play. I should have been pleased to have seen her there and to hear her talk about it. Her papa is very good to let her see so many, though it would have been pity to have denied her. I think you could not well avoid making a visit to Mrs Norsa without disobliging my Lord, and 'tis a thousand pities that a lady that can behave so well should fail in so great a point.

Mr Baldry on Sunday, the time he and his family were at church, has his house broke open and was robbed of above 13 pound, and 'tis but a little while since Mrs Rix's house and Mr Sanders's were broke open the time they were at the meeting, but Mrs Rix had the good luck not to lose anything, for they couldn't find money, and they did not take anything else. Mr Sanders lost but little, poor Mr Baldry came off the worst. Pray give my compliments to Mrs Masters and tell her I wish her good success with her book.

From Barbara Kerrich
Dersingham, 14 March 1750

Dear Sister,

Yesterday sennight I began to wean Tommy, and I think I never knew him a whole week so well. He looks pale still, but I must not expect he should look better for he hath a double tooth just cut through, but at present he seems much better than he was when he sucked. He won't eat anything o'nights but drink plentifully of barley water, and everyday he eat a very good dinner of light pudding, and drink a good deal of best beer. If he do but go on so, I shall be glad he is weaned, I think his flesh begin to feel firmer, and he is a vast deal brisker.

When I have a letter from my mother, I dare say the Dr will do all he can about managing the litter for you, but he says it must be done by some friend at London, as he is wholly a stranger to the person that lets it. Mr and Mrs Bates are going to live at London, he is gone and will be as proper a person to employ about it as can be. This earthquake[169] will make people a little fearful of settling there at present, I am sure I think a great deal about it that am so far off, for I fear it should be more general.

I was prodigiously surprised at the account of Mr Charles Bedingfield,[170] so remarkably religious and good man as he was. I write in haste, I couldn't write last week because the newsman came just as we sat down to dinner and couldn't stay.

From Elizabeth Postlethwaite
Denton, 12 April 1750

Dear Sister,

I shall be glad to hear in your next that you are quite out of danger from the smallpox, and I hope it do to abate here though they still inoculate. Yesterday both Mrs Howman and Miss Berney came out of the smallpox, they think it will prove a good sort. When I talk with Mrs Catherall[171] about going away she was so civil to tell me as the smallpox was in the city, she was sensible I couldn't be at any uncertainty as to the time of going, and therefore should not expect my going at a quarter's warning, but to go when I thought it safest and best.

I have been thinking whether it wouldn't be cheaper for me to send my things by the Lynn waggon than to hire one on purpose. Let me know what Mr Baldry had for carrying your things. He called upon me a little while ago, I forgot to ask him. He complain of not being well. He desired me to let the Dr know that Mr Grimmer was dead that he was concerned with in bond for my brother.

I see by the newspaper that Lord Orford is dead.[172] I think you told me or I dreamt whenever he died, that Mrs Norsa was to live in the house you live in, but I hope it was a dream, for it would be a sad

169. Mild earth tremours were felt in London on 8 February and 8 March 1750 and also in Portsmouth 18 March and Liverpool 2 April: G.M. XX (1750), pp. 88-89, 137, 184.

170. Charles Bedingfield (fl. 1661-1750) of Ditchingham Hall (?), died 14 August 1750 aged 89: Venn, I, p. 124.

171. Elizabeth Catherall was the landlady of Chapel Field House, Norwich where Elizabeth Postlethwaite was later to lodge: Suffolk Record Office (Bury St Edmunds Branch), J750/2 *The Suffolk Mercury or Bury St Edmund's Post* (1725-1728) XVI, 5 July 1725.

172. Lord Orford did not die until 31 March 1751 and was buried at Houghton on 7 April: G.E.C. Peerage, VI, p. 130.

thing for you to have to remove. Here everybody is in very close mourning,[173] instead of grey as they talk of, they are got into crapes and bombazines. Mr Sewell[174] sent this parcel yesterday. Mr Hale desired me to send his compliments to the Dr.

April 13. I had wrote thus far when I received your letter. I am very glad the smallpox is over at your neighbours, and I thought as you do about Betty, that it would be better not to have her run the hazard of changing the air, that I don't design to bring her. Mr Sewell I think, was more unreasonable with me for bringing my things to Norwich, he had two and twenty shillings. I fancy it will be better for me to send by the Lynn waggons. I write in haste for fear I should be too late for the carrier, that I have not time to say any more now, but tell Tommy I hope it won't be a great while now before he will see me.

[On 10 May 1750, John Postlethwaite died as a result of a riding accident – see Appendix 1.]

From Barbara Kerrich
Dersingham, 28 May 1750

Dear Sister,

I had a letter from the Dr last Saturday wherein he tells me he intends to be at home next Sunday. He don't say how he leaves things, only mentions two appraisers[175] from Norwich. I hope the things are not sold, there is several things we really want, and a great many I should like to have: quilts I want, and the white rug I wouldn't have us

---

173. 'Close mourning' or full mourning meant wearing black, generally crepes or bombazines, known as 'Norwich stuffs', for close relations. Short mourning for distant relatives was comparable to the period known as second mourning. It sometimes served as a pretext for buying new clothes. The time span could vary from weeks to months, generally divided into equal parts. Presumably the Kerrich family went into close mourning for Lord Orford because of his family's political influence in Norfolk. He was also Samuel Kerrich's landlord at Dersingham, a more personal connection: Bailey, A. Buck op. cit., pp. 60 - 63.

174. John Sewell also served as a Churchwarden at Denton in 1752: NRO MC 1744/1.

175. Appraisers were laymen (normally between two and four), who were required to draw up a probate inventory of the deceased's personal estate (in this case John Postlethwaite's), before the will could be proved, or in the event of intestacy, letters of administration issued: David Hey, *The Oxford Dictionary of Local and Family History* (Oxford 1997), pp. 6, 2, 114; See below, Appendix I, p. 123.

part with upon any account. The cheese press I would have too, for there is no such thing here, and the plate rack that they drain plates on when they wash them, and a hundred things more I could think on that will come to but a trifle to sell.

And as there is some things to come, they would be of great use to me, and I should like them better than new, for whose sake they were. Sukey is often putting me in mind of things both in the dairy and kitchen that she want, and she desires when you pack up, that you would tie up your things with the linen lines for hers are very rotten.

The Dr said nothing to me how far he has managed these things, but if it be in your power, keep what useful things you can. He said nothing about your coming neither, pray God send us a happy meeting. In great haste.

From Elizabeth Postlethwaite
Denton, 29 June 1750

Dear Sister,

Having leave from you I took the liberty to open the enclosed letters which came on Monday. I wish you had stayed to receive them, for you will see there is nothing to be done but to pack up and be gone.

Though my hopes of staying were but small, yet when I found all hopes were gone it gave me more uneasiness than I thought it would, that I shall be glad to get away as soon as I can. You will see by my mother's letter that she had no answer from the Bishop to any she wrote him about it, that it was quite out of her power 'tis plain to do anything in it. I had a mind to try this carriage before I wrote, but the weather is so cold I dare not. 'Tis a very ugly looking thing but my cousin Johnson say it go very easy that I hope it will do.

The stone-cutter came on Tuesday and put the stone up and altered the arms upon the monument. Mr Sewell was here with him, and asked me whether the Dr said anything to me about getting somebody to preach here on Sunday. I told him no, I thought Mr Kerrich was, but he said the Dr ordered him to get somebody else, who he intend to get I don't know. Mr Chase have been here and all the books are gone, Payn carried them. You had fine cool weather to go home. I hope you had a good journey and found Tommy well.

From Elizabeth Postlethwaite
Chapel Field House, Norwich, 12 August 1750

Dear Sister,

I received both the Dr's letters and I thank him for his kind good wishes, and am obliged to him for managing Slack so well for me.

I performed my journey to Norwich much better than I could expect, but was very weary and my spirits quite sunk, but thank God did not cough which I very much expected, and thought it impossible for me to move so far without, which made me dread the journey. For had I thought I should have come off so well, I should not, I believe, have taken a room at Chapel Field House,[176] but have rested myself at a tavern or somewhere, but as I have, must stay this Winter, for I must pay for half a year if I do not, and that I can't afford to do, especially now Mr Kerrich have used me so ill. For I made no doubt but I should be paid, as he had promised me so often I shouldn't lose a farthing of it. I was sorry to hear the hot weather put you so much out of order, but hope you have quite recovered yourself now. I shall be glad to hear you have, I am weary and must conclude for I still feel my journey. I sent the list of the things you have taken last week, and have here sent an account of things that were left in the house. Mr Baldry have the same. The enclosed letters Mr Sewell sent this morning.

From Elizabeth Postlethwaite
Chapel Field House, Norwich , 24 August 1750

Dear Sister,

I would have wrote last week, but the carrier stay so little a while in town, and Miss Baker of Hedenham just then called upon me, that prevented me. She and her sister were in town all the assize week. Mr Martin Baylie[177] was in town and called upon me twice, and my mother was so kind to send Miss Overton to speak to me. I was a good

176. Chapel Field in St Giles's parish was formerly used for reviews of the city regiment. In 1707 it was railed in and later in 1746 was 'planted with trees and laid out with three useful and spacious walks for the inhabitants by Sir Thomas Churchman,' then the lessee, who appears to have used it 'as a garden or appendage to his own grounds'. In 1754 Chapel Field House was rebuilt for assemblies: Sir Peter Eade, M.D., *Some Account of the Parish of St Giles's, Norwich* (London and Norwich 1886), pp. 55, 321. The present house dates from c.1800.

177. Martin Baylie (fl. 1723-1770), Vicar of Wicklewood 1737-1770, Rector of Kelsale and Carleton, Suffolk 1737-1770: Venn, 1, p. 112.

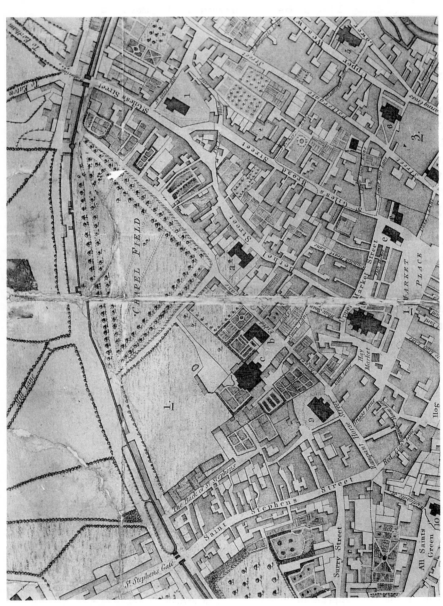

Original scale: '20 chains or 80 rods to every four and seven-eighths inches' – here reduced to 70%.

**Hochstetter's Map of Norwich in 1789
showing Chapel Field House and adjacent area**

Engraving

deal disturbed the two assembly nights with the music and dancing, but it was an amusement to me to see the company, and made some amend for the disturbance it gave me.

My thoughts are often with you and I take very kindly what you mention that what I was obliged to pay here should have been made easy to me, and though thank God I am finely, yet hope I shall be better able to perform the journey in the Spring than I am now. I am sure there is nowhere that I could think myself happier than with you, but am afraid my being with you should be a very great inconvenience as I must turn the Dr out of his study, for he said several times he should not know what to do with his books, and as he will be at a loss where to fix them, my being with you must be inconvenient. Therefore I beg you would speak your mind freely I shan't take it the least ill, or think you value me the less for it, for I wouldn't upon any account have anything happen afterwards that should make any uneasiness between us.

The thirteen pound six shillings the Dr left with me to pay the servants wages and other things with, I here send him an account how I have disposed of it, and that I have in hand now, only one pound one shilling and 3 pence halfpenny, that he will see there is not enough to pay Betty her wages with a Michaelmas, which come to about 49 shillings. She came 3 weeks before Christmas and was to have 3 pound a year. The Dr is very good and kind to contrive so that I shall come into some of my money, and I think Mr Kerrich can have no room to complain or speak against it, it will be strange if he should have the Dr acquainted him with it.

Mr Steygould[178] went to Denton yesterday, I gave him a list of the things I took. The account Mr Sewell took of the things was done that morning I came away, that all things were in such confusion and hurry, and everybody busy, which I dare say was the reason you had not a right account, for to be sure, there was nothing meddled with the time I was there, but what have been done since I don't know. They make sad works in the garden, pull up everything, the skep of bees that was left was turned up and the honey taken out, that how Mr Steygould will find things I don't know. The brass candlesticks I took, but Steygould will send the accounts. There was but little bacon left and it was forgot to be sent with your things so I gave it my cousin Johnson. We burnt two skeps of bees and I have got a good pot of honey here to sell. I sold the hens and the cock, Mrs Baldry and Joe

178. Steygould was the senior appraiser.

Jecks's[179] wife had them, I had 3 shillings for them. I expected to have seen Steygould before I sealed up my letter, but mustn't stay any longer for him for fear the carrier be gone.

From Elizabeth Postlethwaite
Chapel Field House, Norwich, 7 September 1750

Dear Sister,

I have not seen Mr Steygould since the sale. Mr Baldry and he, I find, had words, for Steygould wasn't willing anybody should have anything but the person he carried with him, but Mr Baldry bought a great many things: the 3 servants' beds: the great table that stood in the hall and the chairs in the parlour: and them in my brother's room, and other things. Mr Gooch have sent for the clock, Mr Baldry received the money for that which was 3 pound, and he was at Norwich on Wednesday and brought it to me, and if I keep that I shan't want to take any money off Steygould, nor I don't know whether I shall want that, for I suppose it won't be long before the Chancellor[180] will pay in Mr Kerrich's money, and I suppose I shan't see Mr Kerrich till he come to receive the money off the Chancellor.

Mr Sandby[181] is to come to Denton next week. As you assure me my coming to Dersingham will be no inconvenience to you, I am sure being with you is what is most agreeable to me and where I had rather be than anywhere in the world. And as to your family being large, as I shall have a room to myself whenever I find it any disturbance to me, I can be there. But if it please God my health continue to mend, it will be rather a pleasure to me than a disturbance. Therefore my whole design and intention is to be with you as early in the Spring as I can, for I think it is too late in the year for me to venture the journey now and the days are so much shortened too, that I mustn't think of it, and the weather perhaps will be uncertain, and Slack's carriage is no fence against rain, but am determined to come in the Spring.

Mrs Baldry undertook the care of the cheese at Denton and is to sell them, but Mary made such sad stuff it won't sell for above a penny a pound. I have had the favour of a visit from two ladies that I little

179. Elizabeth Reeves married Joseph Jex 29 Sept. 1738: NRO PD 136/4.

180. Robert Nash DCL (1691-1752), Chancellor of the Diocese of Norwich: Foster III (Early Series), p. 1052.

181. George Sandby (1717-1807), Rector of Denton and Skeyton 1750; Chancellor of the Diocese of Norwich 1768-1807: Foster, IV, p. 1249.

expected, Mrs Howman and Miss Berney, and on Monday she that was Miss Peak was to see me. She is lately married to Mr Gains, the gentleman if you remember it was talked sometime ago she should have had. She and her bridegroom were then a coming into your part of the country to visit a gentleman at Anmer, but she said she could not see you now. I forget whether I told you we could not find the picture of Slack's battle. My cousin Johnson have got the things you desired and will write to you.

From Elizabeth Postlethwaite
Chapel Field House, Norwich, 28 September 1750

Dear Sister,

I would answer your letters of Saturday by the carrier, but he stay so little a while I have not time.

I am obliged to you for remembering my birth, you are so kind never to forget it. I have changed my apartment for one that is more convenient and something pleasanter. You will think it was hardly worth my while as I design coming to you in the Spring, but I avoid by it what would have been a great inconvenience to me in the Winter, which was going into a very cold closet that would almost have given me my death to have gone into it.

I never told you in what manner I live, I am a sort of housekeeper. When I first came I went to the cook's shop, but now I begin to keep fires, I cook my own victuals. I have bought a little tin boiler and little dripping pan, for I roast sometimes, but I am forced to do that upon a string. You would laugh to see my little cookeries, for a little serve my maid and myself.

Slack took the carriage a pieces as soon as I got to Norwich, but he said he would set it together for me whenever I wanted it, and it should cost me nothing, but how he can secure it against rain I don't know. Indeed he may tilt[182] it over with something that will fence better than what is upon it now, but the fore part being so open, which must be so, and there come in most wet that I don't see how it can be helped. I must choose for settled dry weather to come in.

182. A covering of canvas etc.

From Elizabeth Postlethwaite
Chapel Field House, Norwich, 9 November 1750

Dear Sister,

I am sorry your servants are still ill, a sick family is a very great inconvenience and trouble.

I am surprised and amazed at Sukey Brady's[183] behaviour, and her cheating and deceiving you was worse in her than in another servant, for she, I think, was under a double obligation to be just and honest to you, as you had been a friend to her from her infancy. She is a monstrous creature, I am glad you are likely to be better fixed now.

Mr Baldry[184] have brought all the locks off the doors at Denton hither to me. He was here last week and paid me, and he want to know who he is to pay the 5 pound a year to, that he used to pay to my brother for the school, whether Mr Sandby is to receive it. I have had a letter from Mr Sewell and he tell me the Dr have ordered him to pay me the money for the sequestration.[185] I am greatly obliged to the Dr for the care he have taken about it. The Bishop sent a large company of seals, and sent me a letter with them; it was short and sweet. I took it prodigiously kind and as a very great favour.

Tommy will be a pretty little prater by that time I come; I shall love to hear him twattle. I had Mrs Saul to visit me yesterday, she have

183. Sukey Brady went Yarmouth and by 1751 was 'very happily married.' She was joined by her sister Ruth, who said 'she wanted a service so had let herself to a tavern': Ms 588 f. 235 Matilda Postlethwaite to Barbara Kerrich, 11 July 1751.

184. John Baldry was the tenant of the six acres of land bequeathed to the parish by the Reverend Thomas Rogerson, Mathew Postlethwaite's father-in-law. Under the terms of his will of 24 Dec. 1722, their yearly rental of £5 was to be put towards, 'the support and maintenance of a charity school' at Denton. The rent and profits from these two closes of land were to be received and disposed of by the Rector of Denton for this purpose: NRO TER 53/3/12, 20 June 1747.

185. The Denton living was vacant from May until November 1750 between the death of John Postlethwaite and the appointment of the Reverend George Sandby. It appears that the sequestration (or way of managing the profits of a living when vacant) was granted by the Chancellor of the Diocese to Samuel Kerrich, making him responsible for rendering the accounts to George Sandby, Kerrich 'only retaining so much as will pay the Cure during the Vacation and the charge of collecting it'. Mr Sewell collected the monies, giving them to Elizabeth Postlethwaite, who disbursed twelve shillings per Sunday to the Reverend Charles Kerrich for conducting services at Denton. For a full account of this process, see Joseph Shaw, *Parish Law* (1753), Ch. XXVIII. 2. p. 116.

been often to see me since I come. Poor Mrs Dalling have not been well enough I think. It is now about the time for our going into second mourning,[186] I design it on Sunday, I have nothing more to add at present.

From Elizabeth Postlethwaite
Chapelfield House, Norwich, 30 November 1750

Dear Sister,

It was a great disappointment to me my not having a letter on Saturday. I am uneasy about it, fear you should not be well, for I doubt your sick family and nursing have been too much for you. I hope I shan't fail of hearing from you tomorrow. I have been pretty much out of order with a cold but have got it almost off. We have had very pinching weather, and my room is nothing so warm as that I had at Denton.

Mr Sewell was here last week and show me a letter from Mr Sandby, where I see the Chancellor have ordered Mr Kerrich no more than 12 shillings a Sunday. I suppose I must give Mr Sewell a receipt when he pay me the money, but I must beg the favour of the Dr to write one and send me, for I can't make a proper one. He said he should pay me at Christmas, I believe he would be glad to have the money paid him for the school. I shall hear by your next letter whether Mr Baldry be to pay it him.

Mr Baldry have got the distemper amongst his cattle, he have lost one cow, it is very much about there. Payn the Harleston carrier have lost all his. I find he begin to be uneasy about his debt, he happened of Betty in the street and spoke of it to her. Steygould was here about a fortnight ago and valued the things I took, and he said that Page the stone-cutter desired him when he wrote to the Dr, to mention his debt. These are disagreeable things to hear of, it will be a happy thing when all matters are settled and all debts paid. I shall be heartily glad when it's done with, though be not a farthing left for us. Pray what did you give Mr Baldry for carrying your things to Dersingham?

---

186. The customary period of mourning, six months after John Postlethwaite's funeral.

From Barbara Kerrich
Dersingham, 7 February 1751

Dear Sister,

The Dr lately received a letter from Mr Sandby and one enclosed in it from a bookseller at Oxford with a bill upon my brother of long standing, between 2 and 3 pound. The bookseller says he wrote to my brother several times, who wrote him word once that he thought he was paid, but would look over his accounts, and he never heard from him after. If there should be any more bills, the Dr says it will not be worthwhile to keep the estate, for as it is, he thinks we shan't save a penny a year by it, and Joe Jecks says the house must be new tiled.

Mrs Masters happened of your letter where Taylor set up, so took it home with her and enclosed to me by the post. I shall write to her now, but must desire you to get Mrs Nurse to carry it to her, for she didn't tell in what parish or street to direct to her, only said she had taken new lodgings where Mr King formerly kept his writing school.

I have been uneasy for you upon account of the smallpox and wished you here, but now I have reason for uneasiness upon all our accounts, 'tis broke out the nearest house to us where I used to take cream and butter in Winter, and our stables join, which makes it the more dangerous as Martin must go there. I hope God will preserve us, we never were so near it before, not one in our family have had it but the Dr, which is a sad thing.

Mr Steygould wrote this week. He says he saw nothing of the new leather portmanteau last time he was at Denton, only the old one. I should have told you that the Dr wrote to him about it upon seeing in the list that he sent of the things he sold, 'two tables and a portmanteau: six shillings'.

From Barbara Kerrich
Dersingham, 25 March 1751

Dear Sister,

I wrote yesterday by Mr Chase's newsman, who came just as I sat down to dinner, two hours sooner than usual, that I wrote in such a hurry I forgot the chief thing I intended to have said, which was to tell you we shall not be at all afraid of you come as soon as you will.

I told the newsman that Mr Chase or some of his people said they knew nothing about him, the man said he might carry his papers himself if he discouraged people from sending letters by him, so he told Mr Chase of it and he said there must be some mistake, but for the future our letters should be taken care on. Your last letter came by Mr Chase's man, as for Taylor, he come no further than Walsingham this way, and we can't get them from thence.

Tilly and Tommy send their duty to you. I seldom have time for any sort of compliments, but pray give mine to Mrs Dalling and Mrs Saul,[187] and my cousin Johnson and Mrs Nurse. When you come you will see how little time I can spare for writing. I am making a firkin of raisin wine more. Tommy drank all the other long ago, for he drink white wine whey every night.

From Elizabeth Postlethwaite
Chapel Field House, Norwich, 29 March 1751

Dear Sister,

I have received both your letters and I thank you for them, and though I should like to have always long letters from you, but I know the care and pains you bestow upon your little girl and boy leave you but little time for anything else, that I ought to be satisfied with short ones sometimes.

I will certainly come as soon as I can with safety, and I am very glad to hear the smallpox is so soon likely to be over at your neighbours. I suppose you intend keeping that upper servant you have now for us both, Mr Utber said you like her mighty well. Betty have got a spark since she came to Norwich, and I believe will marry at Michaelmas. I am glad you have made some more raisin wine, for I fancy I shall like it better than tavern wine, and it will be a great deal cheaper to me.

I forgot to tell I had a lady called upon me sometime ago, Mrs Medows that live near Ipswich. Mrs Edgar was so obliging as to desire her to come and see how I did, and to know which way I got to Norwich. I believe she thought I had been a cripple, for she seemed surprised to see I could walk about my room, and told me she was glad to find I was so well recovered of my lameness. Here is everybody

187. Mrs Saul, formerly Mrs Anne Farrow, had been widowed in 1747 and remarried the following year. Ms 589 f. 80, Elizabeth Postlethwaite to Barbara Kerrich, 19 Feb. 1748.

very busy after mourning,[188] some people are got in already. Grey silks and poplins they talk will be most worn with black ribbons and black fans and shammy gloves. It will cost me but little for mourning, only a yard or two of ribbon. Mrs Saul come pretty often to see me, Mrs Dalling have never been to see me yet, for she is so often in the way you once see her in at Denton, that she is neither fit to go out a visiting, nor be seen by anybody.[189]

From Barbara Kerrich
Dersingham, 19 April 1751

Dear Sister,

Besides some demands of no great consequence I received one from Mr Barnham of Bungay the other day of near 17 ll. But what gives me more uneasiness than the demand itself is - the first article in his account relates to a bond of 50 ll to Mr Wink of Bungay about 2 years ago. If this should be unpaid, it is impossible to judge how many such there may be, for I have had no notice from Mr Wink about it. I am willing however, to hope both from Mr Wink's silence about any such bond, and the large sums borrowed since that time of Mr Holmes etc, that this bond was discharged by some of those sums. I am to finish this letter but have hardly time, by a letter from Mr Sayer last night, I see Mr Baldry is in haste to have the £5 paid for that Grimmer.

What you thought about this house I fancy was a dream, for we have no reason to think of removing at present. I must send this by the post at last for I hadn't time to make an end yesterday, for I have less time now than ever. My nursemaid have been blooded and a sore is likely to gather about the place, that she has been lame of her arm ever since, which is three weeks ago, and 'tis as bad as ever.

I don't know but it may be cheapest to send your things by the waggon, it will cost about three half-crowns hither from Lynn. I will

188. Public mourning for Frederick, Prince of Wales (1707-1751), who died 20 March. Court mourning was strictly regulated. George II decreed a year's public mourning for Queen Caroline, which in theory was supposed to be observed by everybody. In the case of Frederick, Prince of Wales it was limited to six months: A. Buck, op. cit., p. 23.

189. Mrs Dalling died in 1753: Ms 588 f. 239, Matilda Postlethwaite to Barbara Kerrich, 26 April 1753.

send for a carter in this town and talk with him to know what he will have to come to Norwich for them and let you know, that you may judge when you know about what weight your things will be. This man wants business and will do it as cheap as anybody. I couldn't see him before I wrote now.

From Elizabeth Postlethwaite
Chapel Field House, Norwich, 3 May 1751

Dear Sister,

I am concerned to hear there is still more debts, but I hope that 50 ll to Mr Wink is paid, for I have heard he is a lover of money, and therefore I think would hardly have been silent so long, and the reasons the Dr give make me hope we shall hear no more about it.

I am sorry for your nursemaid's misfortune. I wish your upper maid may stay with you, you gave her so good a character, I dare say I shall like her, and she will be a loss to you, for good servants are not easily met with, and I shall like to have her lie in my room. I have been so long used to it, I don't care to lie without. I have a favour to beg of the Dr and you, that is when I come, if you can with any convenience spare Martin to ride before the carriage. I shall think myself obliged to you if he can meet me at Wymondham. It will do, if it may not be so well for him to come to Norwich. The carter you mention must come with his waggon, if he do come, and let him bring a tilt to throw over the things.

Mr Sayer was here sometime ago, but I have always forgot to mention it, and I surrendered to the use of my will in all the courts where he is steward, but Mr Offley Smith I doubt I shan't see. Mr Sayer said he would, and put him in mind of coming. I believe he don't design it.

Ruth Clark hath sent me my physic since Mr Kerrich have been ill, and in her last letter she said he desired I would send his love and all suitable respects, for he is not able to write a word himself, and it give him a great deal of concern and uneasiness that he have never had a letter from the Dr since his illness. I think to take Mrs Nurse with me when I come instead of my maid.

From Elizabeth Postlethwaite
Benacre, 18 May 1751

Dear Sister,

I write now to let you know the time of my coming home. I set out from hence Tuesday the 29 of this month and shall get to Norwich that night and be at Lynn the next day, where I hope to meet you and should like to get to Dersingham that night, but if you can't conveniently come, let there be a letter for me at Mrs Cooper's. My mother wrote to you last Monday. I hope to have a letter from you tomorrow and that I shall hear how Tommy's physic agree with him. I am going an airing with my lady[190] this morning, that I have not time to say any more.

From Barbara Kerrich
Dersingham, 27 May 1751

Dear Sister,

I find Shimon don't know the way out at St Giles gates which leads directly to Hellesdon. If you go out at any other gates you must go through some part of the city, but it seems St Giles gates are at the end of Chapel Field, that you go past but one house, Mr Suffield's,[191] who have all had the smallpox seven year ago. When you come at Hellesdon bridge, if you go over the bridge it leads to Drayton Heath (the road that we go), and so to Attlebridge where there is a good house to bait or lodge at only - I doubt you can't lie below stairs, they are all brick floors. If you do not go over Hellesdon bridge but keep on the direct road, it will bring you to Sennowe bridge a mile further than Attlebridge. We never called there, but Mrs Gregson say there is a pretty little lodging room below, that's the only good thing you will find there, for I think 'tis a sad looking house. 'Tis 7 mile on this side of Norwich, then you have 12 miles to Mileham, where you will be well entertained.

190. Anne Atwood whose family were merchants in Great Yarmouth married Sir Thomas Gooch, 3rd Baronet, in 1743, when they purchased the Benacre estate. Her portrait by Thomas Hudson was included in the Benacre Sale (lot 146), introduction, note 17 above.

191. Robert Suffield, Gent. wine merchant, died 1753: Patrick.T.R. Palgrave—Moore, 'Norfolk Pedigrees Part Four' in *Norfolk Genealogy XVII* (Norwich 1985), p. 163.

Our man can't be with you on the Monday time enough for you to set out, because of driving his master to Wolferton of Sunday in the afternoon, but he shall come on the Monday and lie at Hellesdon or somewhere near Norwich, and be at Chapel Field House as soon as you please on Tuesday morning. What day would you have the carter come? Let me know in your next, we can borrow a tilt for the waggon. This was but a moderate lie that Martin told your maid, to what he does sometimes, but a lie it is, for his master and he had no words: they were tears instead of words, for Martin cried or seemed to cry all the day before he went away most sadly, and said he must go: so his master paid him his wages, that there never was any thoughts of sending after him, and we hired this man the day after. I can't say but we were all vexed before we knew the occasion, and he took such a sorrowful leave of all his children, and of this family, that I couldn't help tears, but he have left such an infamous character behind him, it would be a scandalous thing ever to take him again. I believe we have got a very sober servant in his place. He was born at Pulham and lived sometime with Dr Broome,[192] but he have lived hereabouts several years.

I desire you would be so kind to pay Mrs Masters 26s and 6d for a pound and a half of tea, and 5 subscriptions. I think it is so, but you may ask her what it is, because the Dr have a notion that some of the tea was paid for, but I think not. I am going to write to Mrs Masters by the post to tell her that you will pay her. If you think you shall be short of money we can send it by our man. Mrs Masters sent her compliments to you in her last letter to me, and said she should be glad to know where you were and how you did.

From Barbara Kerrich
Dersingam, 3 June 1751

Dear Sister,

I received your letter, the carter will be at Norwich by Tuesday noon, and our man too, who shall lie at Hellesdon on Monday night. The Dr will send two guineas by him, if that won't do, let us have a letter from you again on Saturday by the carrier.

192. William Broome LL.D (1689-1745), poet, who assisted Pope in his translation of Homer's *Odyssey* 1725-26, Vicar of Eye, Suffolk 1728-1745; Rector of Pulham 1728-1745: Venn, I, p. 230.

Though there is a bed below stairs at Sennowe, it may be a brick floor, but at Attlebridge there is no bed at all below and your own bed will be warmer upon a bedstead than upon the floor. Take sheets and everything of your own, for she is a nasty slut at Sennowe bridge, and take some cakes with you or something that you like for your supper. I pray God send you a good journey, I shall be glad to see you here safe.

[Elizabeth arrived safely to the relief not only of Barbara, but also their stepmother, who expressed her pleasure at hearing from both sisters 'at once' a few weeks later. Despite her poor health, Elizabeth lived till 1794, surviving Barbara by 32 years.]

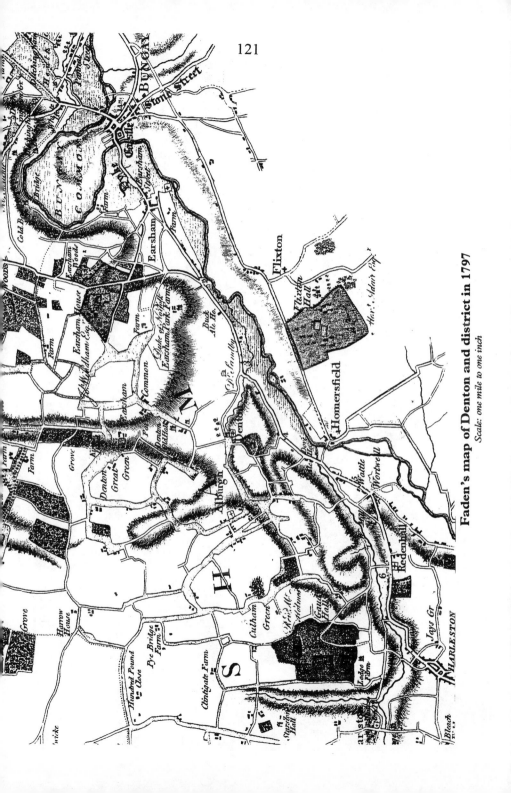

Faden's map of Denton and district in 1797
Scale: one mile to one inch

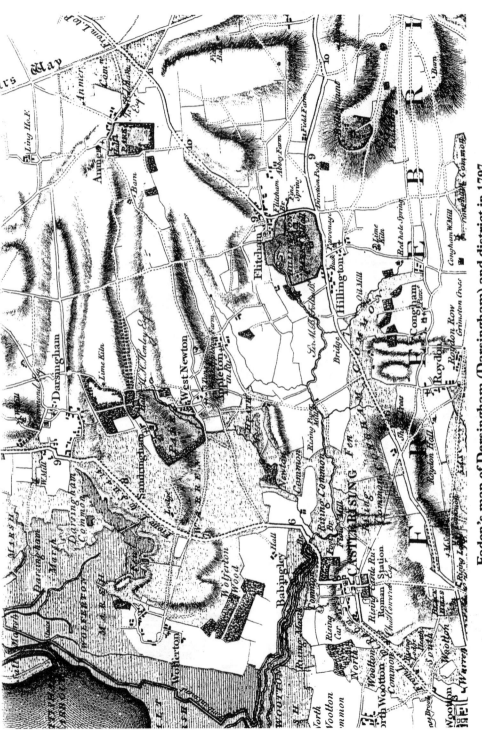

Faden's map of Dersingham (Darsingham) and district in 1797

Scale: one mile to one inch

APPENDIX 1

This exchange of letters between Samuel and Barbara Kerrich clarifies the sequence of events following the death of her brother John Postlethwaite in May 1750, which led to the final break up of the family home at Denton.

Denton
May 19th 1750.

My Dear Wife,
   You will suppose matters are in some confusion here, the accident was so unexpected.
   We have searched diligently, but find no will,[193] and perhaps the demands upon his estate may be more than is yet imagined. I learn from Mr Reeve that he had agreed to mortgage Jecks's farm to him - but that Mr Sayer, who, it seems, knew his circumstances better than any man advised him to sell it, by which we may form some judgement of the state of the case.
   I have sent for two appraisers from Norwich to take an estimate of the effects who are to be here on Monday, and I make no doubt you will agree with me that it will be better to part with what effects can be spared than to load the estate if it can be avoided. I have been thinking of taking the furniture of the best parlour for us, and your sister would have that in the hall chamber and the easy chair; the chairs in the hall are strong, and if you approve of it, I should be for reserving them.
   Your sister is bravely and wishes you were here. Mrs Johnson is with us, I will take all the care I can of all matters. If I should not get back before Sunday sennight, desire Mr Sharpe to supply Wolferton, as I suppose he will Dersingham the Sunday before.
         With all good wishes,
               I am your truly loving husband,

                    Samuel Kerrich.

193. John Postlethwaite died intestate. His sisters were bound in a bond for £200 19 May 1750 to draw up an inventory of his 'Goods, Chattels and Credits' by 31 Aug. 1750, their account to be submitted to the Consistory Court at Norwich by 31 May 1751. By a strange coincidence his father Mathew Postlethwaite had also died intestate in 1745: NRO DN Administrative Bonds for the Year 1745 p. 18; 1750 p. 16.

May the 21st 1750

My Dearest,

I think long till Taylor come to hear how you and my sister do. I write a little before he come, for if he should come so early as he did last week, I shan't have time to write three words to you; pray tell my sister how I am straightened for time, that I hope she will excuse my not writing to her, and it would be little more than form, as she will hear from me by you.

I thank God the children are both well, Mrs Gregson has called upon me every day since you have been gone, and sometimes he, both send their compliments. The man was here last Tuesday about the coach tax, and I set my hand to a little paper, as I saw Mrs Hoste and Mr Gregson had. The money is to be paid next Friday sennight, I may desire Mr Phillips to pay it I suppose, and give him the money, for I can't have answer from you before then. Mr Sharpe preached here yesterday and will go to Wolferton next Sunday. I wish the Archbishop would save him the trouble of going any more, and fix you where you are, but if he won't, one thing I desire we may have, and that is the draught of the house that is in the great parlour; you may easily make the chimney piece good again before the gentleman come that is to have it.

I this minute received your letter and am glad to find my sister and you so well, and wish as much as she I was with you. I should think the furniture would go but little way towards clearing the estate, and there are some things that we must buy very soon if you don't take them. The copper is a good size for us and our mash tub is dropping to pieces, too bad to mend, which I didn't know till t'other day; these things cost a good deal to buy. The bed in the study chamber is better than the bed in your study. We have two or three featherbeds, the tickings are not worth a farthing, and a great many things I could think on, that we want much in the kitchen and dairy and back-house too.

I am very sure you will do everything for the best, but if it could be helped I wouldn't part with anything but the books, for the sake of whose they were, and when you have taken the furniture of these two rooms you mentioned (which I think is quite right), I can't think the rest will amount to much, not near the value they would be to us. The plate to be sure you don't think of parting with.

Tilly desires her duty to you and her aunt and hopes you will think of my little black two armed chair for her.

My dearest, your ever affectionate and loving wife,

Barbara Kerrich

Pray don't forget to take down the view of the house, time enough, for I have a great desire to have it.[194]

APPENDIX 2

By the 1730s growing numbers of clergy and gentry were employing local painters for decorative work and portraiture. In 1734 the Reverend Mathew Postlethwaite commissioned Thomas Bardwell, then living at nearby Bungay, to paint portraits of his two daughters Barbara and Elizabeth and his son-in-law Samuel Kerrich. Delivery of the work proved far from straightforward. Initially Bardwell blamed the delay on the poor quality of the frames from Norwich. These 'he sent back again and hath now some coming from London which he expects within 10 day'. When these failed to appear Postlethwaite went to the painter's house to demand an explanation, but, as he told his son-in-law:

'The painter was not at home himself, but I spake with his wife, who informed me that the frames were lately brought down from London, but that the weather hath been so unseasonable of late, that her husband could not go to work upon them.'

Postlethwaite was not impressed:

'But this I take to be a sham pretence, because both before and since my last to you, he hath been much taken up, not only in drawing pictures at Captain Freston's of Mendham, but in painting the front of an organ very lately set up at Beccles.'

She refused to let him take them away unframed, fresh reassurances were given, but the matter was not fully resolved until July 1736.[195]

Bardwell's career is relatively well documented, which cannot be said of Francis Cufaude's, the painter responsible for 'the view of the house', the overmantel removed from Denton at Barbara Kerrich's insistence. He originally came from King's Lynn, was apprenticed to the Painter Stainers' Company in London in 1722, returning to work

194. Ms 589 f. 195 Samuel Kerrich to Barbara Kerrich, 19 May 1750; Ms 591 f.211 Barbara Kerrich to Samuel Kerrich, 21 May 1750.

195. Ms 591 f. 55 Mathew Postlethwaite to Samuel Kerrich, 14 Dec 1734, f. 56, 17 Jan 1735; f. 64, 7 June 1736, f. 68 2 July, 1736.

in Suffolk and Norfolk by the early 1740s.[196] This view of the
Rectory, a fascinating example of its kind, was described in some
detail many years ago:

'It is a picture in oil...measuring about four feet long and one foot
ten inches deep, giving an isometrical view of Denton Rectory and
gardens, with the church in the distance. It is full of life and interest.
Mathew Postlethwaite and three well dressed women are walking in
the trim walled gardens, and a divine - perhaps intended for Samuel
Kerrich - is riding on a Suffolk punch into the fore-court of the house,
which is enclosed with white railings. There is a "pleasant mount"with
a summer house on the top, as in Jacobean gardens; a smart man in a
scarlet coat and gold laced hat, waves his hand to the people in the
walled enclosures, as he climbs the stile into the wood, and a gardener,
in a cocked hat, digs in the kitchen garden. None of the figures and
objects in the picture condescend to cast any shadows.'[197]

Cufaude also painted two portraits of the Reverend Mathew
Postlethwaite, a small full length and an oval miniature.[198] Perhaps
Elizabeth Postlethwaite had one or other of these copied after her
father's death. (See her letters of 16 June and 19 October 1747, see
above pp. 74, 75).

APPENDIX 3

Mary Masters stayed at Dersingham and among her letters to Barbara
Kerrich is a poem believed to be inspired by the Vicarage garden. It is
published in *Familiar Letters And Poems On Several Occasions
(1755)*[199].The subscribers included, Dr Johnson, Samuel Richardson,

196. M. Kirby Talley, loc. cit., pp. 91-163; for Francis Cufaude, see, Sir Ellis.
Waterhouse, *The Dictionary of British 18th Century Painters* (Woodbridge, Suffolk 1981),
96; Nigel Surry, 'A London Livery Company and its Membership: Norfolk, Suffolk and
the Painter Stainers 1660-1785', in *East Anglian Studies: Essays Presented To J.C. Barringer
On His Retirement, August 30 1995* (eds. Adam Longcroft and Richard Joby) (Norwich
1995), pp. 262-266.

197 Hartshorne, p. 59. The overmantel remains in a private collection.

198. A set of nine drawings in pastel of the Postlethwaite family by John Saunders
(1682-c.1735) were sold at Christie's, South Kensington on 14 June 1982 (lot 127); see
also Hartshorne, p. 9. Their present whereabouts are unknown, likewise the portraits of
Elizabeth and her sister painted by Bardwell. A further portrait of Elizabeth
Postlethwaite also by Bardwell, Christie's, South Kensington 8 Dec. 1982 (lot 103) is
proving equally elusive.

John Hawksworth and Charlotte Lennox. There was strong local
support from Matilda Postlethwaite, the Gooch and Kerrich families,
and as far afield as York - Christopher Peake, and Kent -Thomas
Knight of Godmersham.

Sent to a young Lady in Town, who had vow'd to die a Maid,
in Answer to a Letter, where, in a Copy of Verses, she signify'd her Resolution, and desired an Account of the House and its Situation, in which a new married Lady of her acquaintance was settled. Wrote suddenly at the Request of her Correspondent in a very sultry Day.

A Handsome Mansion, new, and fair,
And situate in a healthful Air;
A rural Garden to it join'd,
With Flow'rs and Fruits of various kind;
Where gravell'd Walks and Beds of green,
Diversify the Sylvan Scene.
In silver Streams the finny Fry,
Here gaily sporting glad the Eye;
At either End a grateful Shade,
By twisting Greens, embow'ring, made:
Where guarded from the hot Extremes
Of *Sol's* insufferable Beams;
We mark the feather'd People's play,
Or listen to their warbling Lay;
Bright Prospects glitter all around,
On rising, or on sinking Ground.
While the fair Meads in fertile Pride,
Embroider'd smile on either Side.
Come then and see this lovely Seat,
So healthful, happy and complete:
Or tell me, from Description now,
Would you not break an idle Vow,
For such a Seat, in such a Shade,
And own the Vow was rashly made?

199. M. Masters, op. cit., pp. 214-215; Hartshorne, p. 60. There is an earlier ms
version of the poem, which includes the line 'Canals too for the scaly Fry': Ms 590 f.74,
Mary Masters to Barbara Kerrich, 3 Feb. 1750.

NOTES ON SOURCES

Manuscript sources

The manuscripts form part of *The Correspondence of the families of Rogerson, Postlethwaite, Gooch and Kerrich 1675-1828,* 28v. inherited by Albert Hartshorne and bought for Corpus Christi College, Cambridge in 1939, Mss 584-611, listed below in numerical order:

Ms 588 Mathew Postlethwaite to Barbara Kerrich 1728-1743
Ms 588 Matilda Postlethwaite to Barbara Kerrich 1733-1759
Ms 589 Samuel Kerrich to Barbara Kerrich 1731-1761
Ms 589 Elizabeth Postlethwaite to Barbara Kerrich 1733-1751
Ms 589 Elizabeth Townshend to Barbara Kerrich 1732-1739
Ms 590 Isabella Barry to Barbara Kerrich 1727-1732
Ms 590 Susan Hoste to Barbara Kerrich 1747-1749
Ms 590 Susanna Houghton to Barbara Kerrich 1739-1747
Ms 590 Barbara Kerrich to Elizabeth Postlethwaite 1733-1751
Ms 590 Mary Masters to Barbara Kerrich 1749-1752
Ms 591 Barbara Kerrich to Samuel Kerrich 1731-1761
Ms 591 Mathew Postlethwaite to Samuel Kerrich 1731-1745

Printed sources (abbreviations)

Unless otherwise stated all books are published in London.

Bailey - N. Bailey, *A Universal Etymological Dictionary* (nd., first published 1738)
Blomefield - F. Blomefield, *An Essay Toward a Topographical History of the County of Norfolk* (11v., 1806).
Buchan - W. Buchan, *Domestic Medicine* (1794).
D.N.B. - L. Stephens and S. Lee (eds.), *Dictionary of National Biography* (63v., 1885-1900).
Foster - J. Foster, *Alumni Oxoniensis: The Membership Of The University of Oxford 1500-1714* (Early Series 4v., Oxford 1891-1892);*1715-1886* (4v., Oxford 1888-1891).
G.E.C. - G. E. Cockayne, *Complete Baronetage* (5v., Exeter 1906)
G.E.C., Peerage - G. E. Cockayne, *Complete Peerage* (18v.,1887-1898).
G.M. - *The Gentleman's Magazine,* 1731-1914.

Hartshorne - A. Hartshorne, *Memoirs of a Royal Chaplain 1729- 1763* (1905).

Harvey - Sir P. Harvey and D. Eagle (eds.), *The Oxford Companion to English Literature* (Oxford 1973).

Sedgwick - R. Sedgwick, *The House of Commons 1715-1754* (2v., 1970).

Venn - J. and J.A. Venn, *Alumni Cantabriensis. Part I From the Earliest Times to 1751* (4v., Cambridge 1922-1927).

INDEX
to Introduction, Letters and Appendices

accidents, 17, 27, 31, 34

Acts of Parliament, 72 and n, 73 and n, 83 and n.

Acton, 57

Adventures of David Simple in Search of a Real Friend, The, 79 and n.

Alburgh, *Norf.,* 44, 95

Ammi, 14, 17 and n, 34

Andrews, Tom, 46

Anglican clergy, 1, 7 and n, 8 and n, 54 and n, 59, 73, 93, 94

Anmer, Norf., 111

Anne, 49

apprenticeship, 37

Arcadia, 77 and n

Arrowsmith, Elizabeth, 10 and n, 15, 16, 18, 24, 44, 48, 55, 64, 88, 90

Arrowsmith, Miss, 10, 24

Arrowsmith, Sukey, 6, 7 and n, 10, 11, 15, 16, 24 and n, 37 and n, 44, 48, 49, 50

Artis, Mrs, 13 and n, 18, 23

Ashbourne, *Derb.,* 60

ashes, 15, 16

assemblies, 10, 26, 31, 109

Attleborough, *Norf.,* 56

Attlebridge, *Norf.,* 118

Bacon, Sir Edmund, *6th Baronet,* of Garboldisham, *Norf.,* 22

Bacon, Sir Edmund, 5th Baronet, of Gillingham, *Norf.* 27 and n

Bacon, Lady, 10, 24, 29

Baker, Miss, 107

Baker, Mrs, 100

Bailey, Mr, 5, 15

Baldry, Frank, 63, 64, 65, 71

Baldry, John, 61, 63, 64, 71, 75, 82, 84, 86, 103, 104, 107, 110, 112 and n, 113, 116

Baldry, Molly, 98

Baldry, Mrs, 71, 109

Bardwell, Thomas, 125

Barnes, Elisha, 22

Barnes, Mary, 49

Barnham, Mr, 116

Baron, Mary, 23

Baron, Mrs, 77

Barry, Biddy, 60, 76

Barry, Isabella, 11, 23, 29, 35, 49

Barry, Kitty, 57

Barry, Lambe, *High Sheriff for Suffolk,* 15, 39, 71, 76

Barry, Mrs, 15

Bates, Mr, 91, 103

Bates, Mrs, 91, 103

Bath, *Som.,* 15 and n, 16, 18

Baylie, Martin, 107 and n
Beaux Stratagem, The, 4, 101 and
n
Beccles, *Suff.,*125
Bedingfield, Charles, 104 and n
beds and bedding, 4, 16, 34, 56,
58, 61, 110, 120, 124
beer, 61and n, 103
bees, 29 and n, 41, 109
Benacre Hall, *Suff.,* 59,67, 86,90,
92, 95
Berney, Miss, 104, 111
Berney, Mrs, 38, 77
Berney, Thomas, *Recorder of*
King's Lynn, 9 and n, 38
Betty, Miss, 26
Betty, 49, 105, 109, 113, 115
Biddy, 31
Blyford, Mr, 72, 93
Blyford, Mrs, 43, 75, 95
Boggas (es), 40, 77
bond, 104, 116
book club, 71 and n,
books, 24, 37, 72, 82, 106, 109,
124
bookseller, 114
Brackendale, *Norf.,* 47
Brady, Betty, 36, 41, 42
Brady, 'Goodman,' 7, 19, 39, 90,
93, 94, 100
Brady, Mary, 36, 42, 88, 90, 94
Brady, Ruth, 7 and n, 42 and n,
65
Brady, Sukey, 7 and n, 83, 88, 97,
106, 112 and n
Brady, Tabby, 15, 18, 19, 36, 41,
46, 47, 63
Brady, Tom, 36
Bramerton, *Norf.,* 77
Brancaster, *Norf.,* 9
Bransby, Peggy, 18
Branthwayt, Miss, 40, 91
Branthwayt, Mrs, 40 and n
Bream, Mrs, 95

Bridges, George, 78
Brock, Roger, 10 and n, 16, 22,
24, 26, 29, 34, 36, 38, 41, 43,
46, 47, 48, 59, 61, 64, 65,67,
72, 73, 74, 76, 79, 83, 91, 92,
93, 94, 98
Broome, William, 119 and n
Browne, Mary, 6 and n, 38, 42,
65, 80
Browne, Mrs, 38, 42, 44, 51
Browne, William, 9 and n, 38
Bungay, *Suff.,* 10, 37, 50, 64, 73,
90, 116
Burgess, Mr, 14, 15
Bury St Edmunds, *Suff.,* 11, 17,
76
Buxton, Hannah, 10, 24
Buxton, John, 22 and n
Calimanco, 38
Cambridge, 8, 18, 26, 30, 40, 92
cards and card-playing, 10, 11, 34
and n, 36 and n, 65
carriage duty, 73 and n, 124
carrier, 54, 60, 67, 69, 85, 105,
107, 110, 111, 113, 119
Castle, Betty, 29
Castle Rising, *Norf.,* 91 and n
Castleton, Mr, 94
Castleton, Sir Charles, *6th*
Baronet, 93 and n, 94 and n
Catherall, Elizabeth, 104 and n,
cattle, 17, 47, 74, 113
Chase, Mr, 106, 114, 115
children, attitudes towards, 13
and n,
chocolate, 14, 59, 87
Churchman, Mrs, 17
Clark, Ruth, 117
cloths, 73, 76
coaches and carriages, 24, 34, 41,
44, 55, 58, 68, 73, 75, 99,
100, 101, 103, 105, 110, 111,
117
Cock, Robin, 79

Coke, Robert, 23
comber, 75, 77
Cooper, Mrs, 118
Coventry, *Warws.* ,60
comfits, 46 and n
cradle, 53, 98
Cremer, Miss, 9 and n, 26, 30(?), 38, 40, 50
Cremer, Robert, 6, 7, 9, 44, 48, 50
Cufaude, Francis, 125, 126 and n
Curll, Edmund, 48 and n
Custance, Mrs, 20
Dalling, Bunning, 6 and n, 9 and n, 15, 37, 55, 57, 67, 95
Dalling, Mrs, 14, 24, 36, 43, 75, 77, 78, 113, 115, 116 and n
Dalling, Nanny, 36, 37
Daniel, 76
Davy, Mr, 27
Davy, Mrs, 42
Davys, Mary, 71 and n
debts, 64, 113, 114, 117
Denton, *Norf.,* Denton Rectory, 2 and n; items removed from, 105, 106, 109, 110; garden, 11, 76 and n, 86, 96 and n; painting of, 109, 124, 125, 126; barns destroyed in a storm, 19; society in, 30, 31; robberies at, 96,103; rental from school, 112 and n, 113; cattle distemper at, 113; Jecks's farm, 123
Dereham, *Norf.,* 54, 60, 67, 69
Dersingham, *Norf.,* vicarage (formerly John Pell's house), 2,72; St Nicholas's church, 8; Pell estate, 9; smallpox at, 40, 114; garden, 47, 48, 77; Whistler's house, 47; robberies at, 97
Diss, *Norf.,* 15
Ditchingham, *Norf.,* 10, 31, 85

Downham Market, *Norf.,* 17
Drayton Heath, *Norf.,* 118
dress, female, 6 and n,16, 18, 23 and n, 24, 26, 27 and n, 29, 30, 32, 34, 35, 37,40 and n, 43, 48, 49 and n, 51, 54 and n, 58, 59, 69 and n, 77, 80 and n, 82 and n, 86; infant, 34, 53 and n, 56, 57,69, 72 and n; male, 42 and n, 67, 80, 82 and n; materials, 6 and n, 23, 29,35, 37, 40, 41, 42, 49, 54, 61, 65, 69, 80 and n, 82, 83, 94, 105, 116
earthquake, 104 and n
Edgar, Mrs, 115
Ellis, Sukey (née Arrowsmith), 55 and n, 64, 72, 73
Ely, *Cambs.,* 93
Ensley, Mr, 96
Exton, Mr, 40
Fairman, Miss, 35
Fairman, Mr, 58, 88
Fairman, Mrs, 58, 88
*Familiar Letters And Poems On Several Occasions,*126 and n
fan, 38, 44, 98
Fanny, Mrs, 91, 92
Farrow, Anne (née Dalling), 39 and n, 55, 74, 75
Farrow, John, 13 and n, 55
Farrow, Mrs, 74
Fereman, Miss, 93
Fereman, Mrs, 93 and n
fishing, 15
food and drink, 10 and n, 14, 15, 20, 24,26, 27, 31, 35, 41, 43, 46, 47,50 and n, 59, 69, 70, 72, 74, 75, 76, 78, 79, 86, 92, 93, 94, 95, 100, 103, 109, 110, 114, 115,119
Folkes, William, 6 and n, 80 and n
Fowle, Thomas, 35 and n, 88

Freston, Captain, 125
funerals, 17, 35, 64, 71
furniture and furnishings, 30, 99,
  100, 105, 109, 110, 112, 114,
  123, 124
Gains, Mr, 111
Gains, Mrs, (née Peak), 111
gallipots, 91 and n, 92,
gardens and gardening, 6, 24 and
  n, 30, 37, 47, 48, 76, 86 and
  n, 126
Gillingham, *Norf.,* 27
Godmersham, *Kent,* 127
Golby, Mrs, 27
Goldson, Mr, 18
Gooch, Anne (née Atwood), 118
  and n
Gooch family, 11 and n, 127
Gooch Hannah (née Miller),
  18(?), 31 and n, 35
Gooch, John, 31, 90 and n, 91, 92
Gooch, Mary (née Compton), 82
  and n, 93
Gooch, Sir Thomas, *2nd Baronet,*
  Bishop of Norwich, 5 and n, 31
  and n, 35,38, 55, 59, 82, 87,
  88, 93, 95, 106, 112
Gooch, Sir Thomas, *3rd Baronet,*
  35 and n, 68, 92, 110
Goodrich, Mr, 47
Goodwin, 31
Great Yarmouth, *Norf.,* 23
Greenwood, Miss, 17
Gregson, Mr, 91
Gregson, Mrs, 2, 38 and n, 40,
  42, 56, 61, 65, 69, 86, 118,
  124
Gregson, Thomas, 9 and n, 56,
  91, 124
Grimmer, Mr, 104, 116
Hale, Mr, 105
Hammond, Anthony, 47, 56
Hammond, Jane , 48 and n
Hannah, 31, 34, 44, 49, 78, 90

Harleston, *Norf.,* 10, 15, 23, 43,
  54 and n, 55, 92 and n, 11
Harleston Cavalcade, The, 22, 23
  and n
Harman, Mrs, 10
Hawksworth, John, 127
Hayward, Mr, 69
Hayward, Mrs,
Hedenham, *Norf.,* 96, 107
Hellesdon, *Norf.,* 118, 119
Hendry, Mr, 50
Hervey, Mrs, 84
History of Miss Clarissa Harlowe,
  The, 6, 83 and n, 84, 85, 92,
  97
History of Joseph …, The, 32
Holmes, Mr, 116
Hoste, James, *Colonel ,*8
Hoste, James, *Major,* 8 and n, 18,
  20, 38, 42
Hoste, Miss, 26, 27, 32, 43
Hoste, Mrs 'Captain', 87
Hoste, Susan, (née Hammond),
  26, 27, 32, 38, 42, 44, 47, 50,
  56, 69, 82, 85, 87, 93, 124
Hoste, William, 42 and n
Houghton Hall, *Norf.,* 4 and n, 9
  and n, 20, 61, 101
Houghton, John, 16 and n, 29, 77
Houghton, Susanna, 11 and n, 16,
  31, 35, 44, 51, 56, 65
Howman, Mrs, 88, 104, 111
illnesses and remedies, 19 and n,
  29 and n, 31, 36, 37, 42, 55,
  56, 59, 60, 63, 64 and n, 65,
  70, 71, 77, 78, 82, 84, 85, 87,
  88, 93, 97, 99, 100, 104, 116
inns and public houses, 10, 95,
  118, 120
Ipswich, *Suff.,* 115
Jack, 82, 83
Jacombe, Miss, 57
Jecks, Joe, 110 and n, 114
jewellery, 42, 59, 80 and n, 82
  and n

Johnson, 43

Johnson, Mrs, 6 and n, 24, 26, 43, 46, 54, 56, 57, 58, 60, 69, 71, 75, 77, 78, 86, 88, 90, 92, 95, 96, 100, 106, 111, 115, 123

Johnson, Samuel, 126

Journey to London, The, 4, 101

Kerrich, Ann (née Manning), 90 and n

Kerrich, Barbara (née Postlethwaite), birth, 1, marriage, 2; grief at loss of baby, 2, 3 and n, 39 and n; discusses fashion, 6 and n, 27 and n, 32, 40 and n, 51, 80 and n, 82 and n; religious beliefs, 7; burial, 8 and n; duties as parson's wife, 8 and n; musical interests, 11, 51; diet, 17; health, 32, 36, 37, 42, 75, 82, 84; pregnancies, 37, 39, 72, 87, 91, 94, 97; stillbirth, 55; birth of Tilly, and Tommy, 4, 51; her garden, 47, 48; literary interests, 79, 83, 97; teaches Tilly to read, 82, 83; problems with servants, 87, 88, 90, 91; portrait 125

Kerrich, Charles, 6 and n, 14, 69(?), 70(?), 94, 99, 100, 106, 110, 113, 117

Kerrich family, 127

Kerrich, Jenny, 43, 67, 68

Kerrich, John ('Jack'), 26, 43 and n

Kerrich, John, 6 and n, 15, 20, 43 and n, 98

Kerrich, Mary (nee Patrick), 39, 43

Kerrich, Matilda ('Tilly'), 2, 4 and n, 51, 53, 54, 55, 56, 57, 58, 59, 60, 61, 63, 65, 67, 68, 70, 71, 73, 76, 77, 79, 82, 84, 85, 86, 87, 88, 94, 95, 97, 98, 100, 101, 103, 115, 124

Kerrich, Mr, 35, 71, 73, 75, 86, 95, 107, 109

Kerrich, Mrs, 34, 49, 98

Kerrich, Samuel, 1 and n, 8 and n, 9, 20 and n, 26, 30, 35, 38, 39, 54, 55, 59, 64, 72, 77, 94, 97, 99, 103, 106, 109, 114, 117, 119, 123, 125, 126

Kerrich, Simon, 13 and n, 23 and n, 26, 39, 48, 93, 96

Kerrich, Sukey, 73

Kerrich, Thomas, 4 and n, 98, 99 and n, 100, 100, 101, 103, 106, 112, 115, 118

Kidman, Charles, 16 and n

King, Mr, 114

King and The Miller, The, 4 and n, 101

King's Lynn, *Norf.* market, 2, 9 26, 65 and n; character, 16; assemblies, 26, 27; fever at, 56; threatened by rebels, 60, 63; mayoral feast, 78 and n; waggons, 104, 105, 116, 117

kitchen utensils, 31, 41, 111

Knight, Thomas, 127

Ladies Almanac, 78

Lakers, Mr, 44

Langley, Miss, 5 and n, 15, 37, 55, 60

Lemmon, Mrs, 96

Lennox, Charlotte, 127

Lindsey, Mr, 37

Little Massingham, *Norf.*, 9

London, 14, 18, 26, 51, 55, 60, 67, 68, 84, 94, 103, 104, 125

Long, Miss, 70

Long Stratton, *Norf.*, 100

Louson, Mrs, 35

Lucas, Mr, 47

lying in, 18, 57

Mansfield, *Notts.*, 60

marriage, attitudes to, 12, 13 and n

Mary, 110

Martin, *Coachman to Barbara and Samuel Kerrich*, 47, 114, 117, 119

Masters, Mary, 101 and n, 103, 114, 119, 126

Medows, Mrs, 115

Melton Constable, *Norf.*, 60 and n

Mendham, *Suff.*, 125

messenger, 20

midwife, 39, 76, 96 and n

Mileham, *Norf.*, 118

Miller, 'Gooden', 47

miscarriage, 41, 85, 87, 88, 93

Molly, 41, 42, 47, 56, 79

Morden, William, 23

Morse, Mrs, 49

mourning, 105 and n, 113 and n, 116 and n

music and dancing, 22, 27, 29, 42, 51, 56, 67, 68, 109, 125

Nan, 59, 67, 68, 90

Nash, Robert, *Chancellor of the Diocese of Norwich*, 110 and n, 113

Nelthorpe, James, 42 and n

Nelthorpe, Mrs, 42

Newgate, Mr, 18

Newgate, Mrs, 18

newsman, 65, 72, 80, 81, 82, 104, 114

Newton, Mrs, 26, 27

Nicholls, John, 64 and n, 93, 94

Norsa, Hannah, 101 and n, 103, 104

Norwich, *Norf.*, election of sheriffs at, 46; fever measles and smallpox at, 56, 104; market, 71; Chapel Field House, 107 and n, 119; assize week, 107, 109; writing school, 114; St Giles Gate, Chapel Field, 118;

Nurse, Mrs, 114, 115, 117

nurse, 51 and n, 76

Overton, Miss, 107

Oxford, *Oxon.*, 58 and n, 59, 114

painter, 75, 76, 125

Painter Stainer's Company, The, 125

Page, 106(?), 113

Pamela, or Virtue Rewarded, 44 and n, 83

Parsons, Joseph, 73 and n,

Paston, James, 22 and n

Paston, Mr, 37 and n

Paston, Mrs, 55, 60

Patrick, Simon, 20

Paxton, William, 101 and n

Payn, 95, 106, 113

Peak, Miss, 34 and n, 100

Peake, Christopher, 127

Peggy, 60

pennyroyal water, 86 and n, 87, 90, 91, 92, 93, 94, 97

Pepit, Mrs, 5, 98

Phillips, Mr, 77, 85, 91, 124

picture, 35, 111, 124, 125

plate, 124

Playter, Mr, 35, 57 and n

poetry and verse, 34, 127

portraits, 74 and n, 76, 80, 125, 126 and n

Portugal, 64

Postlethwaite, Elizabeth (née Rogerson), 1 and n

Postlethwaite, Elizabeth, birth, 1; health problems, 5, 14, 15 and n, 17, 18, 23, 24, 29, 32, 36, 49, 79, 85, 86, 115; literary interests, 6 and n, 85, 98 and n; attitude to religion, 7; burial, 8 and n; pastimes, 34, 37, 43; fondness for children, 41, 44, 57; nickname, 41, 77; offers shelter from the rebels, 63; grief at father's death 60; financial problems, 64, 84, 98, 112;

housekeeper to her brother, 68, 84, 98, 99; her will, 70, 95, 117; prepares to leave Denton, 100, 106; stay at Chapel Field House, Norwich, 107, 111; journey to Dersingham, 118, 120; portrait, 125, 126

Postlethwaite, John, 1, 5 and n, 7, 8 and n, 16 and n, 20, 29, 58 and n, 59, 60, 63, 64, 65, 67, 71,72, 75, 76 and n, 78, 83, 90, 95, 96, 98 and n, 114, 123 and n

Postlethwaite, Mathew, 1 and n, 5, 7, 14, 18, 29, 35, 74, 125, 126

Postlethwaite, Mathew, *of Millum, Cumbs.*, 43 and n

Postlethwaite, Matilda (née Gooch), 5, 10, 15, 22 and n, 24, 30, 31,43, 44, 49 and n, 55, 58 and n, 63, 86, 127

pregnancy, 34, 37, 38, 64, 74, 87, 88 93, 97

Pulham St Mary, *Norf.*, 119

Pyle, Edmund, 60 and n, 87

Pyle, Thomas, 38 and n,

Rackham, Mrs, 71, 88

Ralph, Mr, 54, 55

Rand, Brock, 87 and n

Raye, Charles, 18 and n, 94, 99

Raye, Rebecca, 14 and n

Raynham, *Norf.*, 9, 20, 68

Recruiting Officer, The, 101

Reformed Coquet, The, 71

Reeve, Mr, 123

recipes, 24, 31, 44, 72, 76, 86, 94

Redenhall, *Norf.*, 1, 5, 15, 93, 94

Rice, Mrs, 41

Richardson, Samuel, 126

riddles, 27, 38, 73, 74 and n, 78

Rix, Mrs, 103

St Albans, *Herts.*, 94, 99

Sandby, George, 110 and n, 112, 113, 114

Sanders, Mr, 101

Sandringham, *Norf.*, 8, 20, 26, 40, 41, 42

Sarah (née Shimon), *married to Martin*, 7 and n, 15, 18, 34, 38, 39, 41, 44, 46, 53, 55, 69, 76, 77, 85; their children, Betsy, 85; Billy, 85; Jemmy, 85; Johnny, 41, 42, 43, 44, 46, 50, 53, 57, 79, 85; little Martin, 36 and n, 46, 53, 54, 85, 91; Tommy, 41, 85

Saul, Anne (née Dalling), 112, 113, 115 and n, 116

Sayer, Daniel, 63, 70 and n, 95, 116, 117, 123

Sayer, Muriel , 29

Sayer, Thomas, 24 and n

schools, 11, 12 and n, 113, 114

seals, 49, 112

Sennowe, *Norf.*, 118

Sent to a young Lady in Town, who had vow'd to die a Maid..., 127

sermons, 70, 73

servants, problems, 7; hiring of and giving notice to, 31, 49, 59, 91; misbehaviour, 34, 74, 77, 79, 112, 119; duties and wages, 41, 87 and n, 88, 90, 91, 109, 115

Sewell, John, 105 and n, 106, 107, 112, 113

Sharpe, John, 27 and n, 123, 124

Sharp(e), Mrs, 17

Shimon, 'Goodman', 43(?), 59, 85, 118(?)

Shimon, 'Goody', 34, 60, 75, 92, 98, 99

Shimon (?), Nan, 42, 56(?), 85

Shimon, Robin, 34

Shimon, Ruth, 83, 91, 92, 98, 99

shoes, 36, 43, 44, 51

shops, 41, 111
Shotesham, *Norf.*, 1
Sidney, Sir Philip, 34 and n, 77
Simpson, Mr, 93, 94
Skerry, 47
Slack, 99, 100, 107, 110, 111
smallpox, 37, 47, 49, 50, 56, 67,
    68, 74, 78, 86, 104, 114, 115,
    118
Smith, Ames, 53 and n
Smith, Bransby (née Bransby), 18
    and n, 54, 60, 98
Smith, Charles, 54
Smith, George, 10, 11 and n, 53
Smith, Mary (née Churchman),
    17, 37(?), 53, 90
Smith, Miss, 5 and n, 98
Smith, Offley, 22(?), 117
Snettisham, *Norf.*, 40, 97, 101
Starston, *Norf.*, 5, 10, 15, 18
Stegleman, Mrs, 27
Steygould, Mr, 109 and n, 110,
    113, 114
still, 87, 90, 91, 92
Stillingfleet, Fairfax, 39 and n, 59,
    71, 76, 95
Stillingfleet, Mrs, 39, 49, 59, 76,
    95
Stone, Mrs, 59, 73
Stone, William, 73 and n
Stuart, Charles Edward, *the Young
    Pretender*, 60 and n
Suckling, Dorothy, 27 and n, 57,
    71
Suffield, Robert, 118 and n
Styleman, Nicholas, 64 and n
tableware, 29, 32 and n, 57, 65
Taylor, 22, 114, 115, 124
theatricals, 10 and n, 24
tithes, 35
Toftrees, *Norf.*, 69
Tom, 76
Tom Jones, a Foundling, 98 and n
Topcroft, *Norf.*, 10, 18

Townshend, Charles *2nd Viscount*,
    9, 20 and n
Townshend, Elizabeth, 18 and n,
    23, 30, 31, 34 and n, 37, 88,
    92
toys, 46, 67, 68, 79 and n
Turner, Miss, 35
Turner, Sir Charles, *1st Baronet*,
    17 and n
Turner, Lady Mary, 31 and n
Utber, Mr, 69, 115
Wade, George, *Commander in
    Chief of the English Army*, 60
    and n
Wallis, John, 16 and n
Walpole, Robert, *Colonel*, 9
Walpole, Robert, *2nd Earl of
    Orford*, 99, 101 and n, 103,
    104 and n
Walpole, Sir Robert, *1st Earl of
    Orford*, 9 and n, 17 and n
Walsingham, *Norf.*, 115
Ward, Lady Susan, 96 and n
Waugh, Evelyn, 12 and n
Waugh, Laura, 12 and n
Wetherel, Mrs, 11, 17
wet nurse, 38
Whitsun, Will, 32
Will, 86
William Augustus, *Duke of
    Cumberland*, 60 and n
Wink, Mr, 116, 117
windows, 72 and n
Wodehouse, William, 22
Wolferton, *Norf.*, 119, 123, 124
Wootton, *Norf.*, 48
Wrench, Sir Benjamin, 18 and n
Wright, Mr, 73
Wright, Mrs, 44
Wymondham, *Norf.*, 100, 117
Yeats, Miss, 35
York *Yorks.*, 127